A BUSINESS IN FRANCE

For a complete list of Management Books 2000 titles
visit our web-site on http://www.mb2000.com

A BUSINESS IN FRANCE

Linden Cole

2000

First published in 2009 by Management Books 2000 Ltd
Forge House, Limes Road
Kemble, Cirencester
Gloucestershire, GL7 6AD, UK
Tel: 0044 (0) 1285 771441
Fax: 0044 (0) 1285 771055
Email: info@mb2000.com
Web: www.mb2000.com

British Library Cataloguing in Publication Data is available

ISBN 9781852525835

Disclaimer

This book does not try to direct you towards, nor show preference for, any particular type of industry, organization type, or location, and the author cannot be held responsible for any decisions or investments you make. The financial and legal information in the book is a summary of the position at the time of writing. It is not intended to offer an exhaustive review of these areas, and should not be used for detailed taxation or accounting purposes, other than in the broadest sense. Equally, in a period of economic change, specific regulations may change, and the entrepreneur is ultimately responsible for all actions and decisions pertaining to any business venture.

Having read the book and made your plans, you are invited to discuss your specific business ideas, before taking any decisions about your way forward.

Contact the author via email at Linden@OldKingCole.co.uk

Contents

Introduction

"The French do not even have a word for 'Entrepreneur."
George W Bush

The probable reason that you are reading this is that you are considering moving to France, or you are already here. Whichever the case, you want to start a business here, or improve the one you already have. We all believe that the business we want to start will be fantastic, but reality says that most businesses could do better. This book is written for you.

Now it is common sense that the vast majority of people, if they could afford, would choose not to work. Unfortunately reality takes over, and for many (including some retirees) there is the need to supplement their income – and so starting a business becomes a real option, and it needs to work as well as possible. You may be financially secure, but want to do something that will keep you interested, something to focus on, that gives you a purpose for getting up every day!

The world is full of myths and fables, and certainly there are many associated with business in France. Some people say it is difficult, others complain of specific issues such as Social Charges. Yet people do succeed, and there are many British expatriates working at making a good living here. You could be one of them. There are many differences between business in England and in France, but with knowledge, understanding and application of common sense and reason, there is every possibility of your success.

While life in France can be less expensive that life in England, it is not free, and savings do not last forever. We have met many new arrivals who spend too long treating their new life in France as one big holiday, only to realize too late that even in France you need to earn a living. Also, fluctuations of exchange rates mean that the

9

relative value of your savings can go down as well as up. Few people coming to France find meaningful jobs, even paying close to their UK salary, through lack of absolute fluency in language. French companies would rather employ one of their own. So starting a business is, for many, the only option!

The British have many advantages when it comes to starting a new business in France. We are generally more entrepreneurial than the French (as even George Bush has recognized), less tied to tradition, and there is the added motivation of knowing that there is no real social safety net. You are more driven to success! You may find it hard at times, and are likely to make some mistakes, but with the help in this book, and a positive disposition, you can make it work!

This is a time of change, and there are modernizers in the Government who are trying to move things forward. Changes around the detail are being made all the time, and when you start it would be wise to speak to your Chambre de Commerce and Chambre des Métiers, and these will be able to point out things that may benefit your specific situation. There will be changes, and they are trying to make life easier for new and small businesses. You are not on your own, there is help, so use it.

There is no reason why you should anticipate failure, and this book will show you the things you have to consider to succeed. Businesses here in France do succeed, and there is clearly more diversity and specialism in France than in England. Our own business has been built on good foundations, and is evolving in the way we had hoped. We work hard at what we do, and smart in the way we approach the world of work. We remain delighted and frustrated with being in business here, yet with all the difficulties, we would never go back.

This is not a book about what forms need to be filled in; there are many that can help you with that detail when the time is right. You want your business to be a success, and we can help make that easier. This book will point out many of the things you should know, the general business rules and things that are specific to France. Whatever you choose to do, there is never guaranteed success, but we hope to give you and your business a good start.

As Aristotle is reputed to have said ....

"Where the needs of the world and your talents cross, there lies your destiny!"

1

What could you do?

"Do what you love doing.
As you get older, it will be as important as anything else."

There is no secret formula for success. Business in France, as elsewhere, is all about a good idea at the right time, in the right place, presented correctly to the market, that is thought through to identify opportunities and problems, and you have access to the finances necessary. These finances not need to be large, just sufficient. Luck has little to do with business. Good fortune will follow you if you create the conditions that allow 'lady luck' seemingly to smile down on you. It follows a mixture of hard work, preparation and thought. There is no business that is just right, and guaranteed to succeed. Yet if you do things right, you could have a very good business.

There was once a story I heard of someone sitting waiting patiently for opportunity to arrive at their doorstep. It never came. Instead it passed by various windows, even tapped them on the shoulder, but they were too busy waiting patiently to notice! The morale is that opportunity is everywhere, but it is down to you to look for it! You must make things happen yourself. In France, as elsewhere, when you look you will see opportunity. But you must consciously look for it, see a chance, and make the opportunity work for you.

Doing nothing because of poor language skills (we all face that), no time, and no local knowledge is looking for excuses not to try. Making a business work will require hard work, even here in France.

13

French traders and artisans, the English here, anyone in business, we all work hard at what we do.

France is a delightful country, one that many dream of moving to. When we daydream, we may imagine long lazy days sat in a shady grove sipping glasses of good wine. Many new arrivals in France take time to renovate their home; some take French lessons, and enjoy a more relaxed attitude towards life. It makes good sense to not rush into something without thinking. But the time approaches fast when you must do something. You cannot put off the future forever. There are some important things to consider as you set up your business, these include:

- Your need to be special.
- What are your expectations?
- Your qualifications and experience.
- Working legally.
- Your attitude to work!
- Where could opportunity lie for you.
- Internet and modern technology.
- Common options that have been tried.
- Franchises.
- Buying an existing business.
- Your language skills.
- Help you may get from the state.

Coming to France is not a decision you will take lightly, and there is little or no point in making this fundamental change, only to throw away the opportunity to do something that suits you. Too often in England, jobs get foisted upon us by our age, circumstances, limited opportunity, or the need to take a job to maintain income, home and lifestyle.

This is a life choice, your chance to take the opportunity to do something you enjoy. Not only is it a great chance (and you don't get many), you are much more likely to make a success doing something that you enjoy rather than something that you do just for the money. Being in business is not like a job, is something that is with you always. So enjoyment takes on a far greater importance that otherwise it might. This is a life change, so make the most of it.

What you do will also be determined by your age. As you get more mature, so certain doors are opened for you as others close. Certainly in business you will not want to drive yourself as hard as you do in an employed situation, but you will probably work longer hours in business than ever you do in 'work'. As well, when you enjoy what you are doing, while what you do may be demanding, it seems less arduous because you enjoy it! Work becomes again what it should be, a pleasure and a career.

When thinking about business, consider your family, and close relations you may leave behind in England ... for whatever reason. Your location is important for home, business and family. Your choice of business will impacts your family, quality time and the balance between income and disposable cash, and those things you have around you. Always remember that being in business makes large demands on time, probably more than you would imagine. This will impact family and the result could be stresses you had not wanted. It could also be the best thing that ever happened to you.

Finally, working from home (and many new businesses start from home, even in France), has consequences that you may not imagine. Financially it is beneficial, especially as you can officially charge a realistic rent for the use of office space and phone, and you may be thinking that the move would give more quality time with your partner or children. Yes there are benefits and consequences. We all look for, and are ready to see the advantages of a more idyllic lifestyle, but working from home brings pressures as couples spend more time together.

YOUR NEED TO BE SPECIAL

When you look around you, at the businesses that you enjoy visiting or using, there is always something that you remember about them, something special. It may be the way that the business is portrayed or promoted, the services that are offered, the name of the company that attracts you, perhaps the premises, or even just the personality of the people that serve you.

Even in accountancy and banking, perhaps least interesting areas of business some would say, there will be things you actively choose when picking an accountant or bank. It could be convenience, the way products are portrayed, personality of staff; perhaps even just the décor of their offices, or that their representatives will visit you at home.

Some factors, often irrational, will make you choose one supplier over another. You do business with them, and likewise you will want people to do business with you! I cannot think of anyone who actively chooses to do business because of the boring sameness to everyone else. Why will people come to you, what makes yours a company worth remembering? When you start in business, and in all aspects of your future advertising and marketing, you will want to stand out from the crowd, for all the right reasons. So, as you start to develop your plans, you need to build a very clear image in your mind of what you want your future customers to see.

When you are starting is the best and easiest time to set yourself apart from those with whom you will compete. As it is said,

Be the best, but do not think you are the best!

Unfortunately, when people start in business, they normally look for others that seem to be succeeding, and try to emulate what these are doing – only to make something of a hash of it. It is difficult to spot a good business from the outside, and you could be building in other people's problems. Try to be yourself, and build your business in the way you feel it would be best for you, get things right for you. By copying others you are at best playing to their strengths rather than your own. So try to discover what your strong points are and try to incorporate that into what you do.

Just a note of caution, creativity and personality are great; crazy or stupid ideas can be just that – crazy or stupid ideas! Life, like anything, needs sense and reason. You need to appeal to the majority, or as many as you can within a specific area or industry. Within everything there is sense and reason, and in business you do things for business reasons. There is a big difference between unusual and being crazy. However, sometimes crazy ideas do work, and there is no reason not to push back the boundaries. It will be your business!

WHAT ARE YOUR EXPECTATIONS?

We see television programmes that advocate life in France as free and easy, and it is certainly, in my view, much better, but life here (as elsewhere in the world) is not free! Many new arrivals in France cite the quality of life and the relatively low costs as the reasons they came to France. However you judge these, whatever your standard of living, you need funds. For many, there is the need to generate income, and it seems wrong to assume that the social system will pay for you.

Even for those with an income from the UK, such as a pension, there are many who find that they have need of more funds, perhaps because of poor exchange rates or that renovation costs for property are greater than planned. The excellent health system is not free, you need to pay at the supermarket, and fuel costs money! Whatever, they need to supplement their income somehow.

What you do, and how you run your business, will be driven by what you want from your life here in France, and how this blends with your own personal objectives and desires. You may work part time to start, or for periods of time then not for others. Things may change through time, but if all you expect from a business is to supplement your income and pay for your social and health contributions, the way you do business will be different that if you want to build for children to inherit. Pressures that influence this choice include your age, personality, savings, family, your hopes for their future, regular outgoings and your standard of living.

This will also influence how you best organize your affairs in France. It impacts upon the level of bureaucracy you face and the ease with which you can circumnavigate the punitive levels of social charges. These are known as cotisations (similar to National Insurance Contributions in England) and they pay for state pensions, health and social care. We will deal with this in more detail later, but bureaucracy and cotisations are often given as the main causes of business failure. The simple fact that there is a very broad business base in France, and (it seems) a wider manufacturing sector, shows that these issues can be overcome. I prefer to look at problems as challenges, and things to both overcome and manage, rather than reasons to do nothing.

Naturally, if you set your goals high, you will be more motivated to be businesslike in your approach. There is an old saying,

"Aim for the sun, and you may get to the moon.
Aim for the moon, and the chances are that you will not leave
the atmosphere!"

It never hurts to aim higher than you need, because it is easier to deal with the issues caused by too much work than the problems that not having enough work will generate.

Too much work can mean that you can be choosy with the work you take on. You must work smarter and more efficiently, can even grow the business to overcome the problems that 'being small' can cause. Too little work and the problems are harder to surmount. Bills need to be paid, you worry about finances, your quality of life can diminish, and the authorities still expect their pound of flesh. Even in France, especially in France!

And the odd thing is that those that aim high, and work smart seem to work similar hours to those that have lower expectations! And they appear to enjoy what they do more! There is however greater responsibility, stress, and the need to ensure the work keeps flowing – along with the profits.

If you are working to achieve your own personal and lifestyle objectives, you probably cannot work at income generation 100% of the time. This raises a number of conflicting issues.

- Typically the French authorities seem to assume that you will need to work regularly, and organize their revenue collection accordingly. They will assume you are working, even though you are not, and expect your contributions to continue.

- The other issue is generating adequate funds to allow you both the time and cash flow to enable you work on things that are not business issues, or not work at all.

You may want to find a form of business organization that allows you the flexibility to officially not work 100% of the time, yet pay something towards your contributions so that you can benefit from the excellent social and healthcare systems. This is discussed again in the chapter on setting up a business.

YOUR QUALIFICATIONS AND EXPERIENCE – ARE THEY VALID?

Many people coming to France do so with dreams of doing something different, perhaps trying a business for the first time, or wanting to start a completely new occupation. And why not! You deserve the chance!

The two twin issues of qualification and experience come into play. Obviously the more skilled and experienced you are, the more likely your chances of success. This does not stop you changing direction entirely, and doing something completely different, but you will understand the value of knowledge and experience.

The first hurdle in starting a skilled or specialist business (such as farming or marine engineering, even working as a builder) is proving that you will be able to do what people ask, what can be reasonably be expected you can do given your type of business. In France there is a high status placed on specialism, so you will be joining an elitist group. You will be categorized, and under French law, qualification for your ability to do the work is mandatory.

There is an important concession under European law for those without a specialist background, yet who would like to start afresh. Those from an EEC country with proven experience in a particular field, or who can prove applicable business experience, must be allowed to start a new business elsewhere in Europe. That includes France, so it will be easier (in many ways) for you moving to France to start something new, than for the French themselves (who must be seen to have the right qualifications).

Now, this opens up all kinds of options for the 'would be' business entrepreneur. Yes, you can spend time researching and learning new skills, and gain the relevant diplomas and certificates before you arrive. Or, at the other extreme, you can come, start and learn as you go along! Only you should be the one to judge the relevance of your background, but the greater the potential risk, the greater the potential consequences.

The French are prone to protectionism. A simple way to ensure that any employment is protected for the French themselves is not to recognize comparable qualifications from elsewhere. Hence in France there are highly skilled English nurses, with super British qualifications, that can only find basic nursing jobs, simply because their qualifications are not recognized. Even hairdressers need to prove experience, and find this a possible hurdle. This can be overcome more easily if you start the process before you leave England by making sure you have documents and diplomas to prove your case.

There is another way to prove you have experience – easier than it appears at first. You could show audited accounts from a previous UK business, or have a letter from your accountant (or the Inland Revenue) to back up your claim. Equally you can have signed attestations from past clients, or letters from past employers or partners who attest to your skill. This is usually sufficient. The difficulty the authorities have is in checking on these, especially as the bureaucratic administration of France does not match the lax administration in England.

Here lies a problem with the system. There could be such a paper chase involved, that idle bureaucrats at both simply pay lip service to checks, and anyway there is the language barrier. Yes, obviously we abhor telling lies, but there are many that do not have high morals, and do tell the odd fib. Yes, attestations may be checked, but it is very unlikely errors will be detected, especially if the person writing your attestation actually does have proper credentials. Given distance, lack of real cross-border co-operation, and simple human weakness, the chances of being questioned are slim! However, beware of being too clever. The Law of Sod says that if you claim outrageous experience, without any justification, the person who speaks to you will see through your bluff. It is one thing being clever, another being too clever for your own good!

Given this awareness, surely anyone with the brains to start a business can find ways to overcome the issues and difficulties of proving qualification and experience. But remember, these two issues do go a long way to ensuring success when you are actually in business.

WORKING LEGALLY

Because of the high levels of social charges, there is a vibrant cash (illegal) economy in France. Working on the black (as it is called) is said to account for up to around 30% of the total economy. It seems politically illogical to set such a barrier to being honest, and with high business costs, the authorities actually deter entrepreneurial drive.

Some people come to France with the stated intention of working in the murky black economy. It is especially common in trades associated with building, service industries, and within social networks. The temptations are obvious, and people at all levels and in all areas (dare I say it) have been known to bend to the desire to earn a little on the side, or save a little of the cost of having work done. We have heard that, being pragmatic, some teachers explain to apprentices that they need to earn a little 'on the black' to make ends meet, but not to make it too obvious by doing too much!

While you are in business, you will probably be offered work 'for cash', with obvious implications. Whether you accept or not must be down to you, but do not see this as the main way forward. The high visibility of the English in the French community, and the potentially problems that getting caught can create make it risky. The high costs of the excellent social services have led to empty official coffers, and now efforts are obviously being made to curb illegal working. So any work for cash should be very carefully done, and you should not anticipate this will be your major source of income.

YOUR ATTITUDE TO WORK

Different people have different attitudes to work, and your work ethic will determine your approach to work and life. There is always the difference between working hard and working smart. The smarter you work the less effort you need. Equally important is the apparent French attitude to work, the large number of public holidays, and the

35 hour working week. The problems that this creates for clients, coupled with the long lunch breaks, give the impression that in France little work is ever done!

There are very many French companies that are very busy, and work well in excess of the 35 hour working week so often quoted on British TV and in Parliament; indeed many have so much work that the unthinkable (Saturday working) is practiced. How this is squared with European legislation is a mystery, and how you see yourself relating to this is down to you.

Do not think that the French, especially when they are self employed, do not work hard or long hours also. Indeed, I know some French businesses locally where the business acts as a good substitute for marriage, perhaps the tradesmen do not relish the idea of going home! Married life in France suffers the same as married life anywhere! Remember, the only person who got his work done by Friday was Robinson Crusoe.

LOCATION

Where you will be in France has a huge impact on your business possibilities. We live in Brittany, a farming area with a large tourist industry, famous for its coastline and walking holidays. Close links with England give a large expatriate community with frequent visitors by rail, road, sea and air. These visitors come from all over France and Europe, not just Britain, but ease of access makes journeys from the UK easy and not too expensive. Many are able to speak English to some degree!

Consequently there are many business opportunities for you associated with these markets, directly and indirectly. There is always seasonal work to be had, such as picking vegetables or grapes, but successful businesses are not often built just on seasonal work. The large expatriate community need properties brought to modern standards, and there is work in the building and associated trades. Businesses have sprung up providing English and other food products, and the other service sectors such as hairdressers. Property management, moving agents, translation services, language courses and kennels are but some of the many examples of successful businesses serving the expatriates here. Farming and land is plentiful, and so we have examples of English newcomers who, needing something to do with their spare land, have started pig farms and sell meat products, others have moved into land management, and we even know several English tree fellers, who also supply logs for winter fuel. In other areas of France the mix will be different, and it is important you look at opportunities relevant to where you want to go!

There are some industries in our area where there is already an oversupply of facilities. Many restaurants struggle out of season, plenty who supply food for your fridge or freezer, and accommodation of all sorts is easy to come by. This does not mean that these are areas to avoid, more that if you start a business in food or accommodation, yours will need to stand out from a crowd of others all vying for a limited demand. There are only so many places you can stay, and only so much you can eat.

Some businesses will fall by the wayside unless they are kept vibrant! Beware. Others offer their services in ways that work, but you must not expect that, just because you are different, people will flock to you.

It is clear that each area of France will have different issues associated with it. The Vendee for example, popular as a summer tourist destination, has more seasonal home owners and visitors, with many holiday homes shutting in September. For each area of France there will be a different mix of opportunities. This does not mean that you should exclude areas, but you must realistically consider the opportunities that may exist where you are planning to live.

I am confident, following my own experiences, that wherever I went I could earn a living. You can too, but like me, you will need to become aware of opportunity and the things that influence what happens around you. There is a phrase that says you should 'go with the flow'! It is very true. It is difficult, they say, to push a square wheel uphill, and there are some areas where certain businesses are unlikely to succeed, you must judge this and either find another opportunity or area!

Yet you can do something unusual, especially if what you do is not restricted to (or dependant on) that area. Opportunity can exist bringing new business ideas into an area, but this can be a more risky strategy. An example could be internet cafes, which in some areas work well, but in other areas do not seem to have the same appeal. An internet café in Pontivy has just closed, while another in another town close by is doing well. Why may one work, another fail?

The Pontivy area is quite affluent, has many cafes, is well served with the Internet, and ideal for those of mature years with enough money. The other is less affluent, has more young people, who use computers and the internet more easily, and does not have an abundance of other cafes, or regular meeting places. Because an idea works well in one place, it will not necessarily work in them all. Several months ago my wife and I were in Paris and went walking on a sunny Sunday morning. We stopped for a coffee at one of the few cafes open, an internet café as it happened, and it was full. It served great coffee in large mugs, great muffins, and young people were everywhere. However, there were also many old fogies like me who appreciated just the coffee. Perhaps Internet cafes can work almost anywhere, if they get the mix right, and perhaps the café that closed did not offer what customers wanted, or only limited themselves to people tied to computers!

Nail art is another generally new industry attractive to certain groups, but just because something is popular in England, it does not guarantee success here in France. But it might work! The secret is not what you do, but how you put the whole package together. Things also happen in cycles, and whole industries come and go, almost overnight.

Researching your area is important. You must avoid the same mistake made by a friend, now back in England. He is a great 'spur of the moment' action oriented person who, for various reasons, moved to Brittany with his wife. He had the intention of breeding and selling his pedigree dogs, anticipating a good income as a result, so he said. What he had not considered is that this region is the home of the Breton spaniel, with many kennels, and where the local market for other types of dog is limited. By comparison we know another English lady in our village that breeds flat coated retrievers. However, her interest and reputation in this field was already established before she left England. Something for you to consider!

INTERNET BUSINESSES

Whatever anybody says, the world of commerce is changing, and the Internet has been established as a force in the world of commerce, it is no longer the new kid on the block. This hi-tech media has brought many challenges and opportunities, and is having a fundamental impact on traditional businesses. It opens huge potential for you, for everybody!

Yes, there will always be a need for human contact and service, but with the ability to cut out huge swathes of cost, and the conveniences of shopping from home or office, many are now finding this an interesting form of spare time income, or even a full blown business opportunity. Location in France as opposed to England is possible, perhaps even advantageous if your business is not reliant on one country. Indeed, being in France can open access to other European markets, and breaks the island mentality! As your business grows, location here can even lower your costs.

To show that businesses are exploiting this opportunity while opting for a better lifestyle, a local company is in the process of selling its old carpentry workshop (atelier) to an Englishman with a web based business, and is consequently moving to Lannion to consolidate their business operations there. The relatively low cost storage space for the internet business, compared to England, means that stocking goods and processing orders is less expensive, and the internet business will probably do better in France than the UK! At the time of writing it is not a done deal, but does prove the potential exists!

Many traditional businesses are also seeing e-marketing as one way forward. There are now many websites offering advertising services in France, some bigger and seemingly better than others. E-mail is the essential yet dreaded part of every day, and websites are almost considered a 'must have' in even the smallest business, especially if the address works for you. Could you find opportunity here, bringing your technology skills to France, or use this technology to improve your chances of success?

From another perspective, many have moved here to take advantage of modern communication. They continue their English business from France because technology makes this possible. It highlights how little they are needed in England, which in turn motivates them to come 'across the water'! There are businesses that deal with insurance claims, stock market investors, professional gamblers and even people who run networking businesses based on multi level marketing. What the Internet and computers can do is open up worlds of opportunity, for you and for others.

THINGS THAT HAVE BEEN TRIED

To show the kinds of businesses that have been started, one enterprising individual (Gareth) started a local magazine for the English, The Central Brittany Journal. He also runs a magazine for home schooling. There may be opportunity for you to do likewise elsewhere. I mention this because in the last 5 years the world has changed hugely as more English come and start businesses here. Apart from his monthly magazine, Gareth prints an annual Business Directory for the English locally, and it is this I would like to mention. Covering half of Brittany, this directory focuses on the English market, and includes a huge range of businesses.

Brit Mag, another publication, covers Brittany and Normandy, and is expanding while having been in business only for a few years. Likewise 2 more magazines for the English (Morgan Mag and Brittany Life) exist locally, and all claim to be the greatest thing since sliced bread! They survive because of the English and French businesses that advertise with them. These are now on the Internet too, with others such as Anglo Info.

All manner of businesses exist within the British community. Other than the most obvious, local Brits are now involved with pottery, painting, cafes and bars, book publishing, running campsites, foreign exchange, funerals and repatriation, meat suppliers (bacon is always popular, although some suppliers are better than others), re-upholstery, spare parts for cars, golf courses, library services, book exchanges and English bookshops, music, plant hire, pottery, thatched roofers, satellite installations and security systems ... to name a few. Naturally the building trades are well represented, as are estate agents and property managing companies, journalists, teachers, indeed most trades. However, there is always opportunity, and the large distances involved, high fuel costs, language, and even mixed ability levels of suppliers, makes opportunity seem almost endless! As some businesses start, perhaps from poor advice or planning, whatever the cause, some businesses fail. What is a catastrophe for some can be an opportunity for others, perhaps you!

The English market is perhaps the most buoyant, and easiest to target if you are English, but this does not limit you. The subtle impact that the large numbers of English is having can best be demonstrated by a surprising example of change, given the French love of tradition. An English couple showed enterprise and started a 'fish and chip' van, a mobile service that toured several local markets and did quite well. This has (I am told) recently been taken over by a French couple. Sacre Bleu, It's like taking coal to Newcastle.

How should you react to this? Does the thought of a strong market concern or encourage you? Personally I see the fact that so many have started businesses shows that there is potential, but also that you need to proceed with some care. You must accept that others will be trading, and already be established in the market, although this need not be the case. Perhaps the best way to proceed is to research the area you are moving to, especially the businesses there already, see if there will be competition, understand what they do, and look for opportunities to be different in areas that compliment your talents.

FRANCHISES

Another option you may like to consider, and a sign of the maturity of the English businesses in France, is the growing number of franchises that are on offer, enabling you to benefit from the success of others in business here. Buying a franchise is a very 'long term' and fundamental decision, and these can be found on the Internet or a variety of publications. There are also French property fairs.

Franchises have the start-up disadvantages of being typically more expensive (you pay for the experience of others), and you buy a defined and limited area within which to operate. However, they do bring depth of experience that you otherwise need to learn locally in France, they give support and a support network, have better marketing, a recognized formula that has been seen to work, an existing market presence and a reputation that could otherwise take you years to build up.

You should understand the philosophy of the franchisor (the person who is offering the franchise for sale). All sellers of franchises want cash, often to re-invest in the business, which you can benefit from. Vendors are often as concerned about what you offer the business as they are the price. Why, because their business in that area will depend upon you. So they will train and support you as best they can.

Picking a franchise, if that is your preferred option, is never guaranteed to work. The more effort you put into your choice, the better the decision will be. Here are several things you should be comfortable with, that may aid you with your choice:

- The first golden rule is that you enjoy what you are buying into, because you have less options to change the form of the business through time. Hopefully you will have some complimentary experience to build from. If you start your own business from scratch you can change direction easier, but getting going on your own is harder! It can be a lower risk option to buy into someone else's success; they will not want you to fail.

- The cost of buying into the business is not too excessive and that there are anticipated earning streams that seem at least to be based on the cautious side. Do not be sold on dreams that have little base in reality.

- There is a clear strategy for the business that you can understand, and this has a logic and reasoning you can follow.

- There is a plan for marketing and promoting the business in the area you are interested in moving to, or you are already in, and you are excited by this.

- There is support including training, regular communications, advice, good operating systems, clear investment by the owners, and good financial records showing regular growth.

- What you are being sold is as good as it is presented, and

- The finances all stack up and work for you. This is vital!

You must also get on well with the people who run the business and those that you will be working with. This is much more important than it seems because in a job you can change employers, move or get promoted. Perhaps you can even succeed in getting your boss moved, sacked or again promoted out of harm's way! When you buy into a franchise, you will have invested time and money, but if you do not like and respect the people you work with, you are stuck with (and are very dependent upon) them.

Finally, when you buy a franchise, it can be difficult to re-sell without suffering a significant diminution of value – that is if you can re-sell at all. There could well be a clause that limits your options. But then, looking positively, if it works, buying a franchise could be the best decision you ever made, as several of my friends have testified.

BUYING AN EXISTING BUSINESS

This can seem an easy way into business, because the seller will say that much of the hard work has been done already. But has it, and has it been done well? And if it has, will the benefits that you buy naturally transfer to you.

Be very careful if you buy an existing business, and the first thing you should adopt is a cynical attitude to the whole process. This is an area where there are many pits that you can easily fall into. The first thing to consider is whether you are buying a French business. Remember their characteristic and natural inclination to sell at top price, so beware the price demanded. Assets are often overvalued, sometimes significantly, to support past bank loans.

Do not be beguiled with the opportunity to buy a French business on the understanding that this will solve all your problems of getting into the French market. Unless you are also taking the staff, then as the ownership changes and your face appears, much of the goodwill can disappear. The goodwill factored into the price may be worth nothing to an English purchaser of a French business, as French customers can be fickle to English businesses.

You should also ask why a small business is being sold, and be very wary here also. Businesses are typically sold for two reasons ...

- Because the proprietor is retiring, and has no family line to pass it on, or

- Because there are problems associated with the business – often long hours, inadequate or falling turnover, or the proprietor can see problems coming. Why else would they want to sell? Boredom, frustration, worry, stress, and a plethora of other issues all demand your consideration.

Now, do not be put off by these problems if you think the business is (or can be) fundamentally sound. Naturally the person selling will look to boost the price – it is only natural. Equally natural is your need to bring the price down. What you must understand is the need to be able to walk away, with no regrets, if you cannot agree. If the person will not reduce the price to your limit, walk away. Do not be sucked into paying more than you think the business is worth. And that is bound to be less than the seller is asking – remembering that you have the advantages. You have the money, and the seller wants out!

Equally of 'concern' is the offer to get involved in an English business. If you are offered a business, or share of a business, then you must again ask the question why! If the reason is to find partners to build the business, then you should act as though it were a franchise, and be cautious with your money. If it is because the proprietors want to return to England, then again move carefully and only proceed knowing that you should be able to bargain hard for a much depressed price. Always ask the question ... Why is he selling it?!

Buying an existing business *could* be a very successful move indeed. It is all a question of your belief in your ability to make things work, the value that you can get, and the price that is demanded. Buying any business should be seen much as buying a second hand car, where the seller wants to get top dollar, you want top value, and while the car could be great, you could be buying problems!

WHAT ABOUT YOUR LANGUAGE SKILLS

Think outside of the problems of speaking the language. If you are moving to France, no matter the European Union, you are migrating to a foreign country with different customs and language than the UK, no matter how close the history. The customs you can easily adapt to, for example the guarding of the lunchtime break and that all shops close on Sunday (with just a few exceptions).

The language is another issue altogether, and the ability to be seen making an effort to learn the language brings enormous benefits in the social as well as the business world here. It makes you more acceptable to potential friends and clients, and makes your life fuller. You do not need to be fluent. The better your language skills, the easier it will be to adapt into the French market. There are many examples of where people have set up and made a success, even on the high street, with very limited French, and best way to learn is not in the class, but using what you have, and making the effort. It becomes fun!

English people tend to put all the wrong emphasis on things, and thus make it harder to be clear. A definite fact is that *you* don't hear your accent; you only hear what you are trying to say. To you, your accent is only minor! The tips for easing your accent if you have one are:

- Practice often but do not worry, with time accents soften even though you don't think they do.

- Speak French slower and clearer, because with few exceptions accents soften as you slow down, and as you take the time to say things. The other benefit of speaking slower is that if you speak quickly, natives think you are better than you are, and speed up themselves!

There is a tendency for new starters to try to learn lots of new words and try complex sentences. This is a folly for a number of major reasons:

- If the French think you are better than you are, they will take the brakes off when speaking to you and you will tend to flounder unnecessarily.

- Your ear will probably not work as quickly as your mouth, in that you will be able to say more complex things than you can understand – simply because you have had the time to work them out.

- It is easier to learn to speak French by mastering a few easier phrases, and then expanding your 'word bank'.

- Remember, you will have days when your brain seems to stop working. Or there will be people who you just *cannot* understand, no matter how long you have known them, so don't get disheartened!

There are a large number of English in France who make little or no real effort, and some who make only a token gesture. So if you make a visible effort, you must do better than many and this will be appreciated. Recently I had to visit a French lady administrator in Carhaix. I speak French well enough, even on technical issues, but this lady had me beaten. Could I understand her? Not at all! Worse, as my ear dried up, so did my tongue, but still I persevered, and struggled on. She was fantastic, and very patient. My errors were taken in good humour and at the end of the day, because of my perseverance, I got what I wanted. So it was worth it, and the only cost was a little embarrassment. This experience is quoted because it is recent, but not unusual. The French are generally very patient and helpful, more so than the English when the situation is reversed!

There is another important consideration for why you should learn as much as you can. It involves children and the younger generations, and your relationship to them in your family and the community. Many people are now coming with young children who will go to school or college. There, dealing in French all day long, for lessons and dealing with school friends, children learn the language quickly and well. It becomes natural and they speak French all the time. This is good for them, and increases their future career options.

But beware; it becomes frustrating and unsettling as you cannot understand what your kids are saying, especially if you have to ask them to translate letters for you. It can undermine relationships. So you have to show them that, as they do, so you too are making the effort too.

There are many language courses, and businesses set up to teach the new English immigrants the language. These are of varying standard and effect, and some say people are often best to follow two courses at once! It makes your learning so much richer. Better to have a number of options to learn, rather than rely on one.

Equally valid are the courses that can be purchased over the counter, such as Hugo's 'French in 3 Months' or the BBC's various offerings. These are all very good. Having French clients, friends or French speakers around you is very helpful – provided you interact with them – even if you do not understand everything they say at first. It is also an amazing fact that when having aperitifs, as the volume of alcohol increases, so many English believe they understand French better, and would you believe, the French understand their efforts! What better, everyone is keen to help you, and you will amaze yourself with the speed that you learn the language, even without aperitifs!!!

Many French people speak some English, and with the influx of English people over recent years, and tourists for even longer, and because English is seen as the language of business, a great number of people have made efforts. You would be surprised how many people speak at least some English.

But that does not excuse a lack of effort on your behalf! How many times we have heard the complaints of the number of immigrants to the UK, and their lack of effort to speak English! It is not vital to be 100% accurate because you will find the French will work to understand you if they feel you are working to be understood! What they want to see is you making the effort.

Beware; 'the French' do not like to offer their English with strangers for fear of being corrected and embarrassed. Once they are confident of you, many will want to practice English at every opportunity. This can get very frustrating! If French friends continually correct you when speaking, this too is a compliment. They are trying to help you, although they would hate it if you corrected their efforts.

HELP FROM THE STATE

Do not start a business just to get state aid, nor make your business dependent upon it. Setting out to start your own business is always difficult, but if you need state aid and funds to make it succeed, then something is not right. The only possible exceptions are those in research, and perhaps charities. A commercial operation should stand on its own account, and therefore continued funds should not be essential.

But money is money, and if help is available you would be foolish not to take it. In our experience there is some help setting up in business, but naturally it is not broadcast, especially not to those that are arriving from elsewhere. Equally knowing where to look is crucial. The best place to start is ANPE and Assédic, the equivalent of the job centre and benefits offices respectively. These have now been joined to become 'Pole Emploi'.

There is support for various groups in France. Such groups could include the young, poorly qualified, the older age groups, perhaps single mothers and the unemployed ... or combinations of these. Criteria for support changes between areas and through time, so you will need to ask in your area.

A possible and realistic form of assistance, that will have enormous value during your first year, is to be excused cotisations, which can be up to 25% of your turnover! If you are a subject of an EU state, technically unemployed and signed on, and decide to 'try France' either for work or to start a business, you *may* be eligible for any number of forms of assistance. Check in England before coming! Conditions for help are quite complex and depend on individual circumstances. You must be actively searching for employment, be available for interviews and be ready to work. You must also be completely legal in France.

2

What personal strengths should you develop?

"Believe in what you are capable of doing ...
You are capable of amazing things!"

You are the driver of your future, there is nobody else who is responsible, and if you want to work for yourself, you need to develop a philosophy that says *you* will make that future happen.

You can do it, honestly you can! There is a saying that *perception, not possession is 9/10 of the law*, and if you believe you can do it, you can.

I do not believe in Luck! Yes, you can be fortunate, but good fortune follows people who set themselves up to be fortunate. What is it that they do that makes them seem so lucky! That is what you need to do!

Results come from understanding what needs to be done and making the effort to do it. It is as simple as that, and while there is always a feeling that the face fits or not, clients often are most concerned that you can do what you are paid to do. Also, while initial impressions are important, the most important initial impressions in business are of quiet confidence, re-assurance, easy communication and an image of professionalism. Those who develop these personal skills then set themselves up to be the recipient of good fortune.

You must develop, to the full, your inner confidence. There comes the point where, even if you are unsure how to proceed with a client, you give the client the confidence that you know how to do something, or can easily find the answer. You see, you are as good as anyone else, and have enormous potential. You need to believe that!

Einstein, quite a clever person really I recall, said that he used 12% of his capacity, leaving 88% to go at. Assuming he is about right, that means that the majority of us have the potential to use the 90% or so of our potential that remains untapped. Now if my quote is incorrect, I do apologise, but one thing I know for sure, each of us has enormous potential that remains unused. Now is your chance to do something with it. Give yourself the chance!

If you set your mind to what you want to achieve, and have considered how to achieve your aim, you should be able to get there. Yes, it may not be easy, but things that are worth having are seldom easy, otherwise everyone would already have them. You may not have the world's biggest or wealthiest business, but if you have enough, if you are happy, does it matter?

THE SEVEN ACTION STEPS

No one else will build your future for you! It is not so difficult to do once you get going, and starts with the seven action steps to success! These are:

1. Identify what you want to do

Your list of options could be large. The final decision you make of what business to start will not be perfect. It is virtually impossible for one option to be so much better in every feature, that the choice is obvious. If it is, then that is fine, but probably you will need to weigh up what is important, and how it best suits you. Perhaps the answer is intuitive, perhaps you logically look at a list of points, but whatever you do, at some stage you will need to make a choice.

Starting a business is a little like building a relationship. Choosing a life partner will require that you meet someone, and discover whether you are suitable together. Does he or she conform to some basic criteria that to you are important? From there comes a time of building, when you find out more about your partner, to a point where you take the plunge and decide that this person is the one for you, and together you make commitments into the future. Relationships need commitment to succeed, and you jointly overcome future problems that are sure to arise. There will be problems along the way, and nothing is perfect, but the harder you work at your relationship, the better it works – usually.

Starting a business is similar in many respects; you look at your options, research, make your choice, then commit to it. There is never a perfect partner or business to start with, and try as you might you cannot consider every option. In practical terms you will be pragmatic, or may have already made your choice a long time ago. Always in hindsight you could look back on your choice and wonder "What If", but accepting that no decision is perfect, the time will come when you have to make a choice. Some people find choices difficult, but you cannot start two businesses at once, so you will need to identify several key criteria ..... and choose,

- What is it that you want to do?
- Who else is involved and why?
- Where do you want to do it?
- When are you going to start?
- Why is this the best choice?
- How are you going to proceed?

2. Clarify deadlines

There is a phrase used by some under-achievers ... never do today what can be put off until tomorrow. Your attitude needs to be different and far more positive; otherwise your first day in business will never arrive. You need to decide when you will start, and work backwards from there to decide deadlines when certain critical things should or must be done.

This (in the engineering world) is called the critical path. Certainly there is nothing wrong with beating this deadline, but having set a deadline when things will be done, effort must be made to not let that deadline slip.

France is less pressured than England. Many people come with high hopes, big dreams, and the very best intentions. Of course, as soon as you arrive you feel elated, buoyed and in holiday mood. Yes, make it fun to be here, but remember that resources of time and money are limited, and do not waste too much of either. We have seen people going back to England without following their dreams, saying that the fault is with France, that it is difficult to start business in such a bureaucratic country. Finding excuses is easy, few people blame themselves! Only the other day we met someone who was complaining the problems of getting going, as he had another glass of wine. Wine is very plentiful here.

3. List any obstacles

You would do well to list the obstacles that could arise in any planned action. This is not there to put you off, but to make it easier to face the problems when they do arise. Making a comprehensive list ensures that you have thought of the problems, and equally will consider your options for overcoming them as you progress. This could work for anything that you do, but with larger commitments like moving to France or starting a business, this is a big help.

Having listed the obstacles, you then need to consider if they are important, and what you could do about them. Having done that, a clear benefit is that you are prepared. The chances are that, having thought through the potential problems, they will never arise – and that must be good. Sod's law says that if you have not thought something will happen, it will. The law also says that if you are prepared for something to happen, it won't.

4. Decide the resources necessary

When you are coming to start a new life here in France, and it is a very nice place to be, there will definitely be a need for resources. Money, time, and perhaps some assistance from other people or businesses will be important both for starting your new life ... and your business. Quickly getting into the local support network, getting to know people, will be important too.

Time to get going, or to concentrate on the business, is vital. The property in France, nice as it is, generally costs less than a comparable property in England. There are benefits and disadvantages, but generally the pound or euro in your pocket has more purchasing power when it comes to buying property. However, improving big properties is equally expensive in France as in England, even without exchange rate fluctuations, so do not be fooled into easily parting with your hard earned cash. Look at how much money you have, buy accordingly, and decide budgets for living. Buying a big house means you have big responsibilities when you arrive, that take your mind away from business. Small houses can be just as nice, and can be extended or changed later.

When starting a business, as much as you rely on hard work, you will be equally dependant on the availability of cash. What you need as financial support depends upon what you do and how deep is your pocket. Whatever you do, having insufficient cash can (and often does) spell disaster. Cash flow is King.

You need to know what you expect in terms of business, what effect this will have on your finances, and whether you have sufficient cash and resources to meet all your needs. If you have, that is fine, but if not, what do you need to overcome potential shortfalls.

Sound difficult? Well, the prospect of dealing with business finance often seems daunting, but really it is common sense and very easy indeed. We will be dealing with business finances at many stages through this book, certainly in Business Planning. For these purposes please note that some useful sample forms and spreadsheets can be downloaded at www.OldKingCole.co.uk.

5. Plan the route

If you are planning a journey, the normal thing to do is to plan how you are going to get there! You consider time, costs, convenience, personal preference, type of transport, and even compare providers. It is a natural process you go through without needing prompting or even a list to remind you of what to do. Planning how to start a business is not so different.

Like your journey, start with your destination defined in terms you understand, and your plan is really the step by step process of what you will do to enable you to get there. Planning is never exact, but that does not deny the need for it. Thought now will overcome problems later.

Business planning is the one thing you must not underestimate. The greatest danger to any new business is for the budding entrepreneur to ignore the issue of plans for what you will and will not do. Failure to plan, and you are planning to fail!

Many people, whether they are owner managers or simply self-employed, spend more time planning their next holiday than they do the business that they run for 52 weeks of the year. The basics of your business planning are simple. Later in the book we devote a chapter to it, enough here to mention the priority it needs.

6. Expected benefits

The range of benefits, of being in business in France may be different from those you may expect from being in business in England. In England comes the issue of profits, possibly a nice car paid by the business, perhaps freedom from being told what to do.

Here in France there are many hidden benefits that come from being in business.

Generally you can expect, certainly in the early years here as in England, to make less profit, and to work hard. The question then needs to be asked, are you better or worse off? For reasons I find hard to clearly identify, nearly everyone in business that I meet tells the same story of lower turnover, perhaps lower profits, but more money left in the bank account at the end of every month.

Being in France, and being in business in France, brings benefits that include:

- A better lifestyle and less pressure from issues such as repaying debt. This does not mean that there is no pressure, just that it is not 'in your face'.
- Access to far better health and social care.
- A general acceptance that the quality of life is important, even your clients will care about your well-being.
- You are respected for your skills and enterprise.
- You can expect people to be polite,
- You will enjoy a better lifestyle,

7. *Just do it*

There comes a time when you can expect very little additional benefit from extra preparation, and when you feel the time is right. You just have to get out there and 'do it'. You want to start a business, so the clear and obvious thing to do is start.

France is a country where getting things done can be a little difficult, simply because of language, different systems, officialdom and too many civil servants, and in fairness a slower pace of life. France needs entrepreneurs as does every economy, but it is not made easy for you. But you must overcome this.

You must focus on what you want to do, do it well, and overcome the variety of hurdles that you will encounter. Being in business means that you make things happen and not think that anybody will ride to your assistance like the US cavalry in all those old films. The only person that will ride to your help is YOU!

You will take your future and your prosperity in your own hands. It is then you realise the benefits of your planning, to overcome the obstacles that you will inevitably face, and reap the benefits. And when you do reap the rewards, tell yourself that these came to you because of the efforts you made – and you will enjoy them all the more.

A POSITIVE APPROACH

Many people will look at you and, lacking the courage to do things themselves, will tell you of all the negatives, and all the things that *could* go wrong. All they are doing is justifying their decision to do nothing, they are acknowledging their own problems; they look for all the reasons why they, and you, should not start a business in France. How then do you counter that?

The first thing is to acknowledge that there are many successful businesses in France, and if they can do it, then why can't you? There will be problems, but then ... that's life! Compared to England, France has a selection of industries that are in good shape. Manufacturing is well established, tourism is far stronger, the high street is more vibrant, but is under pressure, agriculture is well established, transport is strong and service industries are many.

There is a lot of opportunity. Equally there is high demand for the traditional skills, such as electricians and plumbers, artists and the arts are actually encouraged, and education is given a high priority.

Do not only consider the obstacles ... there is a great deal in your favour.

The most effective way to make things happen is to stay positive, and recognize negative people for what they are ... Negative. Do not think badly of them, they are just not cut out to start a business and take responsibility for their own futures! It is just wrong for them.

You on the other hand are one step ahead of them. While you acknowledge there will be risks (and that is the reason you have done so much planning, to reduce these risks) you know that you are both capable and determined to make your ideas work. You know that it is possible to succeed, and what is more, you are going to make it happen. The power of positive thinking will give you the edge. If you think you can do it, you stand a very good chance of being right. If you think you will fail ... you are also likely to be right! So stay positive.

There will be times when things do not go well, when results fall short of expectations, when large orders fall through, old clients find another supplier and times when the support you expect from family and friends falls short. Being in business is like every other aspect of life, things go well some of the time, not so well other times. It is at times like this when you need to keep focused on the longer term, and stay positive. You need that positive approach that tells customers that they can have faith in you, and that minor setbacks are just that, minor setbacks!

Get support from family and close friends, they are most likely to tell you of your strengths and are able to see the results to date. Nobody is perfect, and everyone has bad days, bad periods, and makes mistakes. Above all, concentrate on what you have achieved, and look at the things you have done. It is too easy to be negative, and it is a human instinct to ignore or undervalue your achievements ... it is really difficult at times, especially when you are feeling down, to list (or even think of) your successes. But these are what you should focus on.

The fact that you have the courage to consider moving abroad and start a business, progress with the language, develop happy and satisfied clients, a good lifestyle, a nice home, good friends, and a long list of other things that people in England would only envy, is to be admired. Even those that are negative would be the first to enjoy half of what you will have achieved. How many others would have done as you have done, had they only had the courage?

NEVER FEAR FAILURE

The fear of possible failure is often the main excuse for doing nothing. There is a perverse logic to this that says, "If I do not try to do it, I cannot fail. I can always say that I could succeed, but have chosen not to try because..."

Fear is a strange beast, and there is a theory (to which I subscribe) that FEAR stands for False Expectation that Appear Real. How many people are afraid to try something, and then later exclaim that they could not understand why they were so frightened? There is one lady I know that was, for many years, too afraid to go down a water chute. But now, having taken the plunge, spends hours on them every time she visits the pool. The problem with fear is that it is usually undeserved, yet drives people to inactivity for 'fear' of the consequences.

Nothing will last forever, and even the British Empire that appeared so solid has gone the way of so many others. So you start something that goes well for 5, 10 or even 20 years. In Silicon Valley, the home of high risk, hi tech businesses, new businesses come and go with seeming regularity. Times may change, and you decide to change track, or do something else. Or your first efforts do not meet with the success you initially anticipated. Is this failure? No, of course not, it is realism and change. And what is wrong with change. After all, for your own personal reasons, the fact that you are reading this book means that you are involved in change now!

Fear of failure leads to paralysis, inactivity, and brings about that effect that you dread, that your ideas do not work as planned. Fear creates the reality of failure! Let go of the fear and you will start to recognise it for what it is, an excuse that folk have for justifying inactivity!

DEALING WITH DISTRACTIONS

Amongst small businesses in France, and despite what many visitors think, there is definitely a work ethic that drives people in work in France to go to work early, and notwithstanding the lengthy lunch, the French will work a very long day. Yes there is a priority for having a good quality of life, and like elsewhere people do prefer not to work. However, there is a simple understanding here that people need to work to live, and that includes you!

There are dangers that you will need to overcome as you struggle to come to grips with life here in France, most often seen amongst newer arrivals. These dangers include:

- Alcohol – there is plenty of the stuff around – the good quality and relative low price of drink means alcohol is far too plentiful for some,

- Lazy days – often associated with consumption of wine and beer amongst friends, there are too many reasons why not to do what you know you should, it is only too easy to be distracted, and life in France is not one long holiday,

- Letting the language get you down, – finding the French language a barrier becomes an excuse for not doing what is necessary,

- Fatigue – at the other end of the scale, you can work too hard, and become tired. You keep on working, but become increasingly less effective, and

- Losing focus on what you are trying to do, both with your life and your business, becomes difficult – too much priority for the home and your income suffers long term, yet too much time spent with the business and the home and family life suffers as a result!

It is all a matter of deciding what is important to you, and looking to the future rather than just now, and that requires a degree of self discipline. It is important to enjoy the moment, then return to what you are doing for the future. Nobody denies the need for pleasure and fun. It is all about knowing where to stop, and keeping a balance. Should you spend all your time focusing on the future at the expense of today? Of course not, but then the same is true in reverse.

The entrepreneur is someone who lives for now and does things today, but with the future in mind, and you need to take that philosophy to heart!

EFFICIENCY V EFFECTIVENESS

In our village is a man, a Frenchman from Alsace, a very good friend, someone who will do anything for you. Coming from Alsace, he has many 'Germanic' tendencies, one of which is a perchance to be efficient. His time is planned in advance, he has his daily and weekly routine, his garden is organised by the moon, and he is an active and regular participant in village affairs and events. Everything he does is done to structure, and his whole life is well ordered. He is recognised as 'un homme sérieux' in the community.

The only obvious problem with him is that he is inflexible, and routine is all. When things need to change, if the unexpected occurs or he has sudden invites, perhaps outside pressure changes his plans, he feels almost unnerved. He will not, cannot, easily deviate from his schedule. For him this is fine, and as an early retiree, it does not matter that much.

However, as a budding entrepreneur trying to build a reputation, you will realise that your schedule will need to be driven by client needs and times, and what the client wants, the client (within reason) gets. Or they at least must feel that they do. It is especially true with the English here in France, many of whom are on holiday when they come. You will want the work they offer, and as they will only be here for short periods, will try to adapt to their needs.

So, while efficiency is fine, and inefficiency costs money, especially when fuel is involved, in business you need a mix of the two, efficient where needed and possible, and effective in what you do. This latter point is vital in your business. It is up to you to balance the two aspects, and there is no right answer and, equally, no wrong answer.

GETTING THINGS DONE

When you get tired, your energy levels go down and it becomes harder to push yourself. You will see pleasurable alternatives, others around you relaxing, you will face the uphill struggles of being in business, the language will be hard, and from time to time the hours will be long. You are human, and despite the benefits, there will be times when you are fed up. There are also jobs you may put off, like tax returns or getting figures to the accountant. It can become a habit.

Procrastination, the thief of time, is the enemy of all businesses everywhere, especially younger ones. Here, in France, life is just the same, but with seemingly more excuses! These signs of procrastination include:

- You plan certain jobs but never do them, often certain types of job. Difficulties, often real difficulties, can easily be found. These include language, bureaucracy, long lunch breaks, even clients being out of the country.

- You do the easy jobs first, and as jobs keep coming along, those difficult jobs just never seem to get done, and they pile up. Perhaps then they go away as you lose a client.

- You put off routine jobs, because they are simply boring or you dislike doing them!

- You avoid confrontation, often diminishing the importance of the conflict in your own mind, and

- Blaming someone else for your inability to get a job done – the "It's not my fault" syndrome. It's odd how some children seem to adopt this phrase!

Overcoming the problem of procrastination is, like many things, simply developing a good habit and state of mind. It is not hard to turn things around, and be positive:

- Just get started, starting is often the biggest obstacle.

- Again, don't be afraid, like we said, fear is usually imagined.

- Don't put off the unpleasant jobs, in fact do those first to get them out of the way.

- Don't fear failure, relish trying.

- When the job is done, congratulate yourself; even give yourself a small reward!

Being action oriented, getting things done, here in France as anywhere, is a state of mind, and one of the major secrets to building a business. My way of getting things under way is quite straightforward:

- I start now, not tomorrow, even if it is just a small step I am at least underway. Starting is the hardest.

- I seek advice; after all, I cannot be the expert on everything. If I don't know, I ask! The problem here then becomes who to ask?

- Do the least pleasant things first, and do them NOW.

- Do a bit every day, if possible, so that progress gets made.

- Visualise success, and whenever possible get bits finished to easier imagine the end result.

- Give 100% effort in small bursts. It is impossible to give 100% effort 100% of the time, so work hard then rest.

- Make public commitments for when jobs will be finished – it works.

- Do not only suffer, have small rewards, and finally.

- Don't cheat! The only person you cheat is yourself!!!

Different people have their own ways of ensuring progress. These include 'To Do lists' and schedules, prioritisation systems, and taking things a day at a time. Whatever works for you is fine; there is no 'one right way', no matter who says so!

You will develop strengths that take you from being someone who is told what to do, to being someone who knows what is needed, then goes and ensures it happens. If this means you do what is needed, so be it. If somebody else does the job, then fine, but stay in charge. Ultimately you are responsible!

WHAT YOU DON'T NEED!

So you see that, rather than becoming an ineffective person, you become a positive and focused person that sets about building a business and new life in a steady way.

You do not need to start big, you do not need to start on a full time basis, and you do not need a lot of money. You do not need excellent equipment, and you do not need to have every gadget under the sun. You do not need hundreds of employees, expensive advisers, expensive premises, big advertising budgets, and you do not need people telling you that starting business in France is a foolish thing to do. You do not need a million customers, you do not need to be negative, you do not need to be lazy, nor do you need to be clever.

What you *do* need is an open mind, the commitment to make your business work, the drive to overcome the problems you will face ... and you do need to plan what you are going to do.

3

Business planning

*"Never laugh at anyone's dream; people who don't have
dreams don't have much. Concentrate on making your dream
come true!"*

Business Planning is very important, whether you are considering
starting a business or improving one that you already have. The
benefit of going through a structured form of business planning for
the future is not that you end up with a written plan, although that
will be useful to remind yourself of decisions. It does ensure that
you have considered the whole range of issues that will be important
to you and your business later, influencing your future. You set
yourself up in business giving yourself the best chance of success
that you possibly can!

This does not *guarantee* your success, nothing ever does, but it
will seriously improve your chances. Not every business can
succeed, however the biggest cause of failure for new businesses is
(you guessed it) lack of planning.

You do not have to spend forever developing a foolproof plan –
that does not exist. The Pareto rule, better known as the 80/20 rule,
says that you get 80% of the value of planning from 20% of the
effort, and the Law of Diminishing Returns will state that after a
while the benefits you receive from additional planning start to go
down. This does not imply that you should not do any planning, just
that you should judge the best time to stop planning and do!

In planning, the Pareto rule can be applied in a variety of ways. 80% of your problems will come from 20% of your customers, as will 80% of your profits, though not necessarily the same 20%! If you have staff, 80% of your problems, absences, customer's complaints will relate to 20% of your employees, again not necessarily the same 20%. And so on. While you may be incredulous, it seems that this is one of life's most common ratios and applies to life generally. Try it yourself, perhaps with friends. Ok, it may work 70/30, or 85/15, but as a generalisation, 80/20 is easier to remember, and it works!

While you want to do the best job possible, planning into the future must always contain an element of guesswork. However, you should do what you can to ensure success, not 'trust to luck'. Luck has nothing to do with business; success is all down to preparation. What sort of things should you consider and develop in planning your future in business:

BUSINESS BACKGROUND

This overall section of your business plan is a summary of the detail that appears later in the plan. I am often asked why you should consider a description of the business in your planning. Like any good book, the introduction is developed last. You will only know how to describe your business when you have fully been through this business planning process, and know what you will be doing in more detail, your specialities and strong points, and where you want your business to go.

When you know the background of the business, you will be surprised how often you will mention or discuss it, often with clients. This does two things, to inform and influence people, and motivate them to choose you and your business over others, to become your clients. You have one chance to influence people and their decisions, and it has been said that the first minute is vital to do this. Imagine the limited impact when you describe what you do in bland facts ....

- "Oh, we do decoration."
- "Yes, you can leave your pet dog/cat with us."

- "We do curtains/fix computers/do B&B/sell English foods."

While all of these things could be true, possibly adequate descriptions of your business roots, do they describe your priorities, your experience, your past clients. Would they generate enthusiasm and confidence? Would it make someone choose you? Imagine what else you could say:

- "We do offer a complete service should you need it, but specialise in decoration and finishing, offering advice, and help with choice of colours." …. Whatever suits your skill and the situation of the moment,

- "Yes, we will look after your pets while you are away, and you can go with confidence knowing that they will be well looked after. I am sure they will feel right at home," … Whatever you feel would give that owner confidence, you may even have separate runs, more space, even perhaps (as some kennels do) radiators for cold winter nights, that is what makes you different and special,

- "We specialise in making curtains to measure in a range of fabrics/solve the problems people are having with their computers and take away the worry and inconvenience/can put you up in a room that offers …./can provide you with the English foods that you miss in France that include …."

To use words with ease and fluency that will interest and positively influence the client, you will need to have thought through why the person you are speaking to should choose you. What do you offer, and what could you offer, that makes you different? What do you think your clients will want and value, and how can you stand above the competition in their eyes? To do that with any degree of confidence requires that you have thought about it! Of course, you then have to live up to high expectations, but that is another issue!

Other issues you should include in your business plan are…

YOUR PERSONAL CREDENTIALS

In your business planning, you must consider your skills, your strengths, and what you bring to the business. This is not an opportunity just to bash yourself by listing all your weaknesses, it is an important time to be positive, look at your own specialities and strengths, what makes *you* good.

Do not underestimate yourself, nor deny successes that you have had, that you perhaps take for granted. Your interests, commercial beliefs and priorities, what you have achieved, all these and more should be included, as well as your life's achievements. The natural habit and tendency of the majority is to sell yourself short, rather than puff yourself up. Many people like to hide behind a curtain of under-achievement, not put themselves up for scrutiny. Successful people acknowledge but do not concentrate just on weaknesses; it is your positive aspects that will make you strong.

On this last point you should use this as an opportunity to direct your development, how to take advantage of your specific skills and overcome the areas where you consider you have possible weaknesses. It is a brave person that acknowledges shortcomings, but it is a winner that overcomes these shortcomings while taking maximum advantage of their strengths.

It is amazing how few people can list out areas where they are strong. This may be a part of the British psychology that tends to concentrate on reasons why not to do something, or reasons why we might fail! It is a source of amazement to me that so many people have such a low opinion of themselves!

A way of overcoming this is to take several sheets of paper and list out a number of things, perhaps with the help of somebody close, things you have done, or talents you have. Every little achievement. Perhaps they could do it as well! These areas include ...

- Areas where you have succeeded – including marriage, children, driving, qualification and education, languages, DIY, sport, indeed any aspect of your life.

- Good experiences you had at work, in all areas of your working life, however small and seemingly irrelevant it may seem, including promotions, travel, responsibility, indeed anything that has given you pleasure and made you feel good about yourself!

- Personal skills and tendencies, including character traits, friendships, and how you deal with a crisis – to name but a few!

We all have weaknesses, and we can all concentrate on these if we wish, but concentrating on why we should fail does not give use confidence to go out and succeed in business. You need a positive attitude, and that stems from how you see yourself!

The reason for all this is simple. It makes you understand that you are a much stronger and vital person than otherwise you may think and, knowing this, you will be better able to communicate this confidence to future clients. Nothing gives others more confidence, than you being confident of yourself.

HOW MUCH FINANCE IS NEEDED, AND WHY

One of the most important aspects of your planning is finance, as this will direct the way you start in business and how you will proceed. Obviously this is one area where you need to initially consider things in general terms, and then revisit throughout the planning process to understand whether something can be afforded! Finances and their limitations is something to be aware of, always, which is why it is included here.

Typically those starting in business feel some things are essential. Certain aspects of equipment may be needed to do certain jobs, and you will need to consider whether you have the funds to afford this. Be cautious in what you buy, what you spend money on! It is amazing how often that expensive equipment once considered vital is now unused and has tied up large amounts of cash.

On a similar vein is the need for new cars, expensive offices and the plethora of business life that other people in business try to sell you, things they try to convince you are vital to your success. You need to ask whether these things are essential to your success or theirs!

Some years ago I was asked by a friend whether he should change his car, and what kind of car he should get. Money was tight, yet he had made the mistake of stopping to look at a nice car. Friends had said that his car was perhaps too old and did not have the right status. At the showroom the salesman pounced, as the salesman is trained to do, and had convinced him that a new car was essential. He was still in two minds, hence his question to me. We talked around this issues of what he needed the car for, the benefits and weaknesses of his current vehicle, the costs of keeping the current car and of the new, and the needs of financing. He kept his old car because his finances did not really allow the extra commitment.

The French do seem to have a more practical attitude to usefulness and utility, and you will see many French people that keep assets while they have value. The French do tend to consider the impact on business finances before they purchase, and having purchased a new asset they then look after it. You will see French people keeping cars for many more years, and generally being much more cautious than in England. Perhaps the ease of credit in England over recent years, even the encouragement to spend, has been at the root of this. Money spent on unnecessary purchases of whatever kind does have to be repaid.

Forecasting business finance is critical, and there is a section on it later in the book, here it is enough to understand the general parameters you are working within, and then later, when you have worked through your finances, understand where you will see high points and problems. That way you will have considered how you will deal with them.

YOUR FOCUS IN GENERAL

Whether yours is a new business, or you are looking to improve an existing business in difficult times, it helps to clearly understand the focus it has. Yes, there are general areas of business that are largely determined by your skill and interests. This could be 'electrics and plumbing' or 'catering', car mechanics or gardening, building or carpentry. This simple description is not enough, and breaking it down further focuses on where you need to concentrate, and adapt your business accordingly!

Decisions that will be of general practical interest and importance to you include ....

- Location – will your business be general (such as an Internet business), trading across borders or between areas, or will you be more concerned with a local or specialist market. Location can also have an impact on costs, so you should consider this when setting up, in that certain areas are less expensive than others. One specific reason why so many businesses are run from home is that this reduces or negates the costs of premises. Certain areas of France (regeneration areas) give incentives for new business start-ups, often through reduced corporation tax.

- Local in France is different to local in England. France is much bigger than the United Kingdom, and despite the roads being better/less busy/straighter, the distances involved can be considerably bigger. This has an impact on transport costs, delivery, the ease with which people can come to you (and their costs etc), accessing materials, marketing, and dealing with specific groups (such as the English settlers) or industries (such as tourism). It can also impact the time taken travelling between places, which must be accounted for. A map on your wall with circles showing rough guides of how far you will travel, or cost bands, may help.

- Age groups vary, their needs change, and opportunity exists within this for you to provide for the needs of people at varying ages. In Rural France, the needs are more marked. Older people find things very difficult given travel restrictions and distances. Yes, social care can be excellent, but shopping and cleaning, gardening and other 'heavy' jobs they can find hard. Younger people also have differing needs, and they have disposable income! Focus your business with care, because how you contact the groups you pick, will determine your success.

- Sex always raises itself, but true to form in France as in the UK, the needs of women and men vary, and opportunity exists to provide for the needs for both groups. Hair care is always a need, and there are services, industries and shops that target women's specific needs. Flowers are a frequent gift often given for the pleasure ('juste pour le plaisir'), nail art is becoming visible in some towns, and services that help women at a variety of levels are often seen, certainly within the French community.

- There are very distinct and separate groups across France, which should be considered as separate markets, and they need to be approached and treated differently. These groupings include :

  - Nationality groupings such as the English or other Europeans, the French dominions (DomToms), and others. A far higher importance on nationalism means that the crossing of national groupings is more difficult without some form of integration and grasp of language. Being a part of a group brings advantages, but also a dependence on the vibrancy of that group and its purchasing power. When the exchange rate between Pound and Euro changes, for better or worse, the impact this has on French businesses that appeal to the English market is immediate. Try not to be too reliant on one sector!

  - The French are a nationalistic group unto themselves. They tend to be patriotic and prefer to support French businesses. What a national strength, that England lost many years ago under years of poor government! Breaking into this (French) market is not easy, but can be done! Linking to certain important companies or groups, or building good friendships with locals can help, as do business contacts with French companies. You can make inroads using or selling through local markets.

- Language groups – many French people speak some English, more than you would imagine when first you meet them, but English is not the natural second language everywhere. Latin roots to French means that in the south of France, Italian and Spanish is wider used than in the north, in the east of France German is more common. Alsace has a separate language as well as French as a second language and German a close third, and in Brittany there are several forms of Breton, which has the same status as the Welsh language in Wales. France is a big country!

- Selling to industry groupings such as winemaking, fisheries or agriculture have clearly defined and specific issues affecting them, and are more defined in France than England. Farming especially has a strong political powerbase, and it infuriates the English as to why Westminster cannot be as strong for England as Paris is for France!

- Regions, Departments and Communities are much more important simply because of tradition. The local community has a far higher status in France than England. The politics of local government in France as well as the sheer size of the country emphasises this.

- Your direction determines how you advertise and communicate, as does the nature of what you do. The ease of communication with your chosen market may influence where you decide to live in France. If you look to advertise within the English speaking market, where you live will limit your options. Some TV satellite installers, for this reason, will travel the length and breadth of France to work. There is the old phrase that you will go to where the work is, and having set up a business, you will suddenly become more aware of this and pressure. Where we live there are many available routes for advertising, but in other areas they are perhaps not there – although an opportunity could be to find an area with many English and no English language publications ... and start one yourself.

- The distinction of whether you are a supplier to the trade, perhaps as a subcontractor, or whether you deal with the client direct will have a bearing on how you market and charge for what you do. People visiting France as tourists see little of industry because it is often located in a 'Zone Industrielle' and is less obvious. You could find opportunity helping French companies address better the needs of the English speaking market, or even teaching English as a foreign language (TEFL).

YOUR OVERALL AIMS

Without a mental picture of where you want to be, you stand no chance of getting there. Imagine you are going on a trip, and you are the driver, the first thing you need to know is where you are going. You will look at the map; probably decide where you want to be by when (perhaps to stop for lunch), and then plan the rest of your trip accordingly. To hit your target for lunch you will then have a good idea where you should be at certain times.

Your goals for business are just like this. You will specify that (ideally) you will have reached certain points along your chosen route for company development by a certain time, or at a certain cost. These points could be profitability, turnover, market share, products you are able to offer, even just starting your business by a certain date. There will be things you want to achieve; these will be your objectives. To work, objectives must be more than just good ideas and give you a warm 'cuddly' feel, they must be clear and specific, otherwise they probably will not work.

Objectives should be **SMART**, an acronym for

- **Specific** (they are clear and precise, not woolly and vague),
- **Measureable** (you can therefore see your progress by measuring how far you have progressed),
- **Achievable** (they are not pipe dreams, you know you can do it with your best shot),

- **Realistic** (they relate to what you want for yourself and the business), and
- **Time-bound** (there is a definite time when you will have achieved your objectives, and will have earned a reward). This last point is often forgotten; with the result that action needed towards achieving your objectives also gets forgotten in the blizzard of daily activity. My objective for completing this book was targeted for Mid October, and as the date draws closer, so the pressure to finish grows!

PRODUCTS AND SERVICES

What do you plan to do? Remember, products are things you offer for sale, and services are what you do for the client to help that sale. Sometimes the distinction is very clear, a car salesman offers a new car – that is the product – and the service offered makes the whole experience of buying enjoyable or not! Sometimes that distinction is less clear. In a restaurant the product is a meal, the service is everything that makes it a pleasurable experience. In insurance, the product is the policy, the service is everything else associated with the process of selling and maintaining that policy, and everything linked to the relationship you have with the client.

Let's look at a few examples. A travel firm sells a journey; a theatre sells an evening's entertainment or a 'show', as do the radio and television; a decorator sells a finished project, look; a supermarket sells the whole experience of buying your range of products from other manufacturers; a hospital sells the repairs needed to your body; a government office sells the range of 'services' that they are set up (and paid) to provide; a water company sells clean water; an energy company sells energy. Each has a specific product they were set up to provide, and they are judged both on the quality and price, and the service they provide in association with this.

So let us do away with this issue of 'Service Industries', unless we are talking about things like 'Tourism' or 'Travel' and the like. When you are talking about your business, you will be selling something specific, and that is your 'product', and the service associated with that is a much more personal thing altogether. Where this is important for you is in knowing what you are supplying for the customer, the product, and how you are going to make it easy to buy from you, the service!

A potential client will not come to you unless they have a very definite need for something. This is what they are buying, although that product may be somewhat intangible such as information. The service aspect are the associated issues that relate (and have importance) to that client. Other examples (other than the car) could include ...

- The meal out – the product is the meal, the service issues could include waiting on table, decoration, setting, opening hours, even the type of food and it's quality.

- Education – the product is the course itself, the service aspects could be educational support at home, ease of access, aids and accessories, even practical aspects to increase learning or understanding, or that the course is run in English and/or French.

- A holiday – the product is obviously the holiday, the service issues include all forms of assistance including information, support in travel arrangements, heath insurance, even having agents where you are going to make the stay more enjoyable.

- A newly decorated room – the product is the fresh décor in the room, but the service could include advice, moving furniture, timing, indeed a plethora of things that cost you time or money, and that you need to build into your costings.

WHAT MAKES YOU UNIQUE?

What is it that you offer, that sets you apart from your competition! Why are clients choosing you? Obviously they want something, but why from you? It may seem a silly question perhaps, but it has some fundamental connotations. Why did they pick your advertisement?

Do they know of you? Were you recommended? What reputation do you want to build?

The services you offer, and they way you present them will set you apart from your competition, for good or bad, and invariably this will have a cost. We have moved to a more service driven world, and your clients have a higher expectation of the services you will provide in addition to the product that is purchased. No longer can we have the Henry Ford philosophy that you can have any colour, as long as it is black.

In France, certainly within the English ex-patriot community, there are a range of services that have become standard, such as dealing with French suppliers when language issues are raised. The many English second home owners also may have specific needs. Work for this group may entail things being done while they are in England and you may feel that good communication, pictures and updates via the internet would help and benefit them.

What makes you UNIQUE – your unique selling proposition (USP)?
What do you offer that your clients would value?

Having looked at what it is you do, and the services you offer, you now are able to compare your offering to the public against your competitors and determine what makes you special. You have developed your Unique Selling Proposition.

The benefits of having thought about this come when you are talking to clients; you simply bring this into the conversation at an appropriate time. If it helps to close the sale then this has done its job!

Of course there will be things your competitors do that are different to you, that makes them special, and we have got to hope that your package is more attractive than theirs.

THE FUTURE – HOW THINGS MAY EVOLVE

You should consider how things may change in the future. It seems difficult when you are planning to start a business to want to consider changes, but things do happen, and the pace of change in this world is speeding up. Change can be forced upon you, but it pays to have considered the sorts of changes that *could* occur and their likely impact when you start. What sort of things could we be talking about? This list could prompt you:

- **Economic changes** – for good or bad, economies change. Sometimes money is more plentiful, people want more things and are prepared to pay more, or have jobs done that might seem like luxuries. Other times the reverse is true. There are many 'Brits abroad' who have assets and money in the UK, and rely upon the transfer of cash, or they have fixed pensions. Naturally if the exchange rate varies adversely, their position in France can become tenuous. Many though cannot afford to return, unable to sell their homes. Change may have adverse consequences, or open opportunity.

- **Technological changes** – things move on, times change, you get competition or things you do may become outdated or begin to lack sparkle. Everything has a time limit. New products come on the market, and leave again. Equally true, this can make older technologies fashionable. Who would thought that in France the Citroën 2CV would achieve almost cult status? The whole aspect of technology has created a sector that tries to maintain disappearing skills. The emphasis on use of chemicals to improve food production has resulted in a industry that looks to more traditional (biological and organic) methods and even the rejection of anything 'unnatural'.

- **Novelty** – the latest marvellous idea can soon become outdated, like last year's fashions. Economic pressures, time or changing tastes can cause this, as can copycat suppliers flooding the market, them charging less and making it hard for you to make a profit.

- **Boredom** – one of the things to guard against is to start something that does not really interest you, which does not fulfil you. If this happens, then longer term the business will not really survive. It is one thing for the clients to be bored, quite another for you to lose interest in what you do!

Whatever you see may happen in the future, and you will know better than most, try looking ahead to what these changes may be.

YOUR MARKETING PLAN

Whilst you understand the direction your business will take, very business needs to plan it's marketing in greater detail, and the following section is your 'Marketing Plan'. In some ways it is the most important part of your planning. In the main it is just looking in greater detail at those things that have already been touched upon earlier. The points raised in this section are not exhaustive, but they will make you think about and decide your customer base, and how you relate to them.

1. Your market place

- **Description of your market** – Look at your local situation and describe in detail the market you want to specialise in. You may show preferences, you may put limits on (say) how far you will travel. However, you need to consider just where you want to trade!

- **Who will use you?** – describe both a typical and a preferred customer, if they are different. You may already be trading with one group, but want to trade with others. This will focus how you should be marketing and communicating. For example, if you are advertising French lessons then there is little point advertising on French radio stations, your clients will not be listening! You may already be teaching the English, and see an opportunity (again) teaching English as a foreign language (TEFL?), in which case using French media is vital.

- **Why?** – Ask yourself honestly why people use, or will use you. Your Unique Selling Proposition in relation to the markets you serve may (or may not be) applicable. If it is not, then you may need to reconsider how you are selling, who you are selling to, whether the product is right, or whether there are things you should be doing that you are not!

- **Major customers/clients (either by name or type)** – If you have, or are anticipating major clients, people upon whom you do or will depend, then note them down. How much of your business will rely upon them? It forces you to realise your dependence if things change. You may deal with a certain group of people, for example the English, or rely on a certain skill, again for example sewing or pottery, but are there other things you could do (such as running courses, opening a shop and stocking other things as well, or whatever)? What will be the impact of this, how will it benefit you?

- **Buying patterns and order sizes** – when people buy from you, ask yourself the question how much they will buy, and how often. It will help you plan your sales, how you sell, and all the calculations that will stem from this. For example we see people selling small carved items, and you could ask how many of these people would buy, so how big is your marketplace? Also ask yourself how you will deal with the subject of 'more work'. Having got a client, there are always more things that can be sold, either in your line or not. You can always introduce other products or trades. Why do this? It is easier to sell more or other things to an existing client than to find a new one. Again, if you give work for other trades, possibly they will introduce you to additional work also. Between nationalities this does not work as well – the French tend to introduce French contacts, no matter how many times you may introduce them to yours!

- **Any seasonal issues** – You can be assured that in almost every industry there are changes during the course of the year that are just due to the seasonal changes and holidays.

Just what these are will, of course, depend upon the industry you are in, and your client group. What you would imagine and what actually happens are often different, and you will not know for sure what to expect until you have been in business for some time.

2. The competition

- **Who do you compete against** – you need to understand exactly who you will be competing against, and what their strengths and weaknesses are. This has several benefits, and certainly helps you develop your service items and how you communicate with the market through advertisements.

- **Comparison of products and services** – Compare yourself to the competition, and look for similarities and differences. Why? Well clearly you are looking to see where you have an advantage, and how best you can present yourself. Also, if everybody is chasing the same clients, they may be missing opportunity elsewhere, as soon as you know that, your chances become clear. Typically for the British in France, there are products that are not being exploited, and groups that are missed.

- **Why do clients use you?** – One of the hardest things to do is to ask your customers for their opinion of you, or even ask what they want. Although communication here can be limited, asking what clients see can be illuminating. You would be surprised the range of views, and how they differ from your own perception.

3. Marketing and sales

- **How do you compare to your competition** (in quality, price, service, image)? – It is not always easy to find out specific details from competitors, unless you come across them when bidding for contracts, or you occasionally use them yourselves or do work with them. You can guess, but like most small businesses, hard facts are rare. Still, try to see how clients see you relative to others.

- **Pricing policy** – do you have one and what is it? – How do you build up your charges, what are your priorities, and do you have any structure that you use. If you do, what is it? There are standard costing systems across a lot of French industry, especially in the skilled trades, so that competing purely on cost is rare between French firms. It emphasises the importance of reputation and service. Of course, English companies do not know the system in many cases, meaning that they are often cheaper (not knowing the full implications of charges) … and can struggle to survive at first.

- **What about product or customer support?** – In France, as in England, there is an expectation of a guarantee. This is not a problem, and the vast majority of legal traders and artisans are insured, either for minor works (2 years) or major projects (10 years). However as a quality supplier you will be keen to ensure customer satisfaction; and it is less costly in the long term to provide good customer support.

- **Advertising activities** – Just what advertising will you look for, what will be your budget, and what do you expect as benefits. Are there any low cost options when you start? How will you assess whether the advertising has been successful? Advertising is important, but spending the earth on advertising is not an option. You need to ensure that your advertising is effective!

- **Interest shown by prospective clients** – Has there been any interest shown by prospective clients in what you do, or what you plan? Too many people walk through life anticipating that everybody thinks the same as them, and will show the same interest in your offering as you do, and are therefore bound to use your services. The question then rises of whether people will part with cash for what you provide. There is a world of difference between an expression of interest, or even pleasure, and a willingness to part with money! The main people (not all) who make money at craft fairs are the organisers and caterers!

- **Who sells for you?** – As unpleasant as some people find the idea of selling, every small business needs to sell to survive! Some clients will come to you and will buy, but you will need to sell (the next job, another garment, a second biscuit, whatever). Also, you need to get a client to part with money for what you do ... and collect that money when it is due.

OPERATIONS PLANNING

You must consider not only what you do, but also how you intend to do it. It is all very well you liking something, even having done it as a job. It is quite another starting or running a business in the same field.

When we first started in France, we did some work for a friend's mother. Looking back it was a great experience to understand how much we would need to increase our pace if we were to do this work professionally. Professionalism needs both the right attitude, you need to look like you have done this many times, and have the confidence to match. If any of these is lacking, you must think how you will overcome your shortcomings.

A way around this is to price the job, not the time it will take to do the job. That way, if you are slow, it is you that is losing.

Some other things to consider include ....

- **Dependences on key materials and labour** – Do you rely upon any one supplier? The question needs to be asked what you will do should that supplier let you down. You cannot build your future on one business without having a contingency plan if things go wrong. In France, especially in the period between July 14th (Bastille Day) and the start of September we have the period of annual madness, when everyone has their holidays. Other than for tourists, effectively France closes. Typically supplies will be disrupted, suppliers close and stocks are (naturally) run low, and you can have problems even if the supplier remains open!

- **Critical points regarding capacity**   (including facilities, plant and equipment, labour) – Like it or not, there will be people and things you do depend on. Perhaps these are French customers or colleagues who can introduce you to 'the French way', or suppliers who are perhaps less reliable than others, or just certain pieces of equipment. You may face the situation that some people will help, but only for cash, giving you the problem of how to account for what you give them! Whatever the situation, you need to understand what the problems might be so that you can plan for them. Just understanding where the problems might arise is often half the solution.

FINANCES AND RISKS

The essential lifeblood of business, after sales, is money. You use it to buy things, you are rewarded for your efforts by money (in the most part), you probably require this income to live, and you acquire assets by using money. If you do not have enough to pay your debts, you have problems!

In business profit is key. Equally important is when those profits arrive, and what you do with them when you have them. Your level of profitability depends upon what you do, but without making a profit your business is doomed. Equally, while you may expect profits to be a certain percentage of your turnover, you will never be absolutely sure of this until you are paid, and then at the end of your financial year. Over the course of each year, you should follow your income and your outgoings, and have a good assessment of how you are proceeding. Do this and if things are going wrong, are not to plan, you stand a good chance of knowing why and then putting things right. Leaving it until the end of the year is fatal.

The ideas associated with finance are not difficult, and with computers the traditional problems of working out forecasts and assessing progress through the year are simplified to the point where business finance is really quite easy.

There are several aspects of your financial planning that you need to be aware of ...

- A summary of the key data and forecasts for the flow of cash. Later there is a chapter devoted to financial issues. Typically it is your finances that are used to measure your success, and allows you to judge the effectiveness of your business – and any problems that may exist.

- Trend of sales. Sales drive your business – not just the number of sales but their value. If the trend of sales is upwards, and you are making profits on your sales, then all is well. Taking seasonality out of the equation, if the trend of sales is downwards, or you are making insufficient profit on what you are selling, then you have a problem.

  When we concern ourselves with this, we need to try to forecast our profits based on the sales we envisage we will be able to generate. Of course you say that you will not know exactly what your sales will be, but you will have a good idea. You will know your fixed costs, you will know how much profit you can make per item, and so by comparing your ideas of sales and costs you will be able to calculate what your profit should be. Is this enough? If yes, fine, if not, what do you have to do to improve?

- Cost patterns are always something you need to understand. Obviously profit is the reason you are in business, and you must know your costs to find your profit. Now I hear you say that this is obvious, but it is not always the case! Indeed, few smaller businesses actually know their costs, both their direct costs (although these are easier to track) and general expenses. In many small businesses the issue of costs is akin to a black hole.

- Breakeven – There is a section in this book about 'Breakeven', in the chapter about finances, that point in your business where the profit you have earned on sales covers all of your costs over the year, and you move into profitability. The benefits of this are best explained in the section devoted, but here it is important to understand the need for adequate sales to cover your costs before even considering profits.

- Cotisations and Tax. Cotisations, better seen as National Insurance Contributions as the UK equivalent, are very high in France and cover social charges, state pensions and health service costs. Taxation seems less arduous, both personal and corporate. Cotisations are set at a percentage of an individual's earnings, are charged on profit in a larger organisation, and taken as a fixed percentage of gross profit in a micro-entreprise (with the assumption here that your gross profit will be around 48% of turnover excluding material purchased). There is more detail in the section about finances, it warrants you learn about the implication of cotisations as they affect your business, as it is vital you know what they will be, *and* when you need to pay them! The reason is simple; the authorities want this money as you trade, whereas in England they wait until the end of the year for assessment. You cannot delay paying them in France, as they fund the social services!

- Capital Investment required. You will need to have a healthy idea of what money you will need to invest to buy equipment, and when you are likely to need it. This will depend very much upon your plans for the business coupled with your financial projections. When planning, at any stage in your business's development you should be aware of any likely drains on cash, and therefore are aware of what you can do to overcome any problems. This impacts the flow of cash that was discussed earlier.

- What money you will need to take out of the business regularly as wages, so that you do not live on the company's money. Keep your money and the company money separate!

71

OPPORTUNITIES AND THREATS

In life there are always opportunities and threats, and what you need to look for are ways that your business can develop, opportunities that may present themselves, and where problems may come from in the future. Being aware of potential problems is important, and goes a long way to overcoming them before they even arise.

- **Opportunities** – these exist for everybody, but two things influence the number and value of opportunities that present themselves. Experience shows that opportunities only arise if you have created the possibility that allows them to arise. Secondly, you need to be looking for opportunity, and be looking in the right area! By trying to identify opportunity in your planning, you are not looking to identify *every* opportunity that may present itself, you are conditioning yourself to look for opportunities in general, and indicating areas where you *think* they may be!

  Opportunity is often best looked for in response to downturns or changes in the market. In France there are many reliant on the English, both visitors and residents. Both groups rely upon exchange rates, and when this goes down, spending power is seriously reduced. When exchange rates change adversely, almost before it has happened you should be looking for ways to adapt.

  Nothing stays the same forever, and we live in a world of change. Part of your role must be to keep your eye on trends and 'think on your feet'. All businesses go through a similar cycle. It is tough to start, then you have an easier time when you have become established, then things start to get tough again as markets, products and fashions change. To stop that being a major problem, when times are good, you should be looking for either new opportunities, or ways to freshen what you do.

- **Threats**, risks and potential problems are all very similar, in that they have a negative impact on your business. Dealing with threats is much the same as looking for opportunity, if you try to see where they are, you will be better prepared to deal with them as they arise. Looked at positively, opportunity, problems and threats are the same thing seen from a different perspective.

We come full circle. There are always other things that you could consider, including why you came to France in the first instance, your health, family, commitments and a plethora of issues that are important to you. All these will influence your business.

There is never a perfect plan and no planning can be 100% accurate – that is like reading the future, and unless your name is Doctor Who, seeing the future is difficult indeed. Yet Business Planning is very important and improves your chances of success. The benefit of what we have discussed is not just that you end up with a written plan, but it does ensure that you consider the range of issues that matter to you and your business.

And finally, remember the issue of advice from others? Listen to others, learn, and take advice, but ...

Don't believe all you hear, or say all you want to!

A wise man learns from the mistakes of others.

4

Setting up your business in France

*"When someone asks you a question you don't want to answer,
smile and ask them why they want to know!"*

Any business activity in France must be registered and requires a
legal structure. There are three alternatives:

- You can be registered as an individual operator, self
  employed, like a sole trader, a 'Micro-Entreprise' for tax
  purposes. The new 'Auto Entrepreneur' is just a simplified
  version of this.
- You can be registered as a company/corporation, even as an
  individual.
- You can be recognized as just doing casual work through the
  Cheque Emploi service – an official way of paying casual
  workers that ensures that their contributions are paid!

The most common route is to start business as a Micro Entreprise, or
sole trader as it is best recognized from the UK, as this is by far the
simplest and easiest way forward when you are new to the country
and the world of business here. For some it is not appropriate, and
this chapter sets out your options and the implications of your
decisions.

A word of warning. One problem you will face, irrespective of
the kind of business you form, is the sheer volume of official
paperwork that you can expect when you start. Most asks for money,
and looks official. Many are irrelevant, however some are very

important, and must be dealt with. Just throwing everything away knowing that important items will be re-sent is not an option.

Accountants are a help here, as they seem to have an official role of dealing with French administration, acting as 'middle men' on your behalf. You must make your own mind up as to whether you want to use an accountant. For me they are worth their weight in gold just to deal with officialdom, but they can cost you around €1000 per year, so you need this in profit from your business just to cover their costs! It puts pressure on you to have a business bigger than you think necessary to cover your personal needs!

There are people who have set up in business to help new arrivals. Their help is often good for home based and family issues and questions. Others have set up to help you start a business, and deal with the associated paperwork in French. This *can* be an expensive option as their help can often be available for free. All new businesses are expected to attend a week long business course to help you set and run your new business. You should attend one anyway, and in Dinan in Brittany it is run in English – so English attendees will understand it! Your local 'Chambre de Commerce' and 'Chambre des Metiers' are really helpful, so ask them for help!

There are several expensive mistakes that are commonly made by British people looking for tax efficient businesses, and the three most common are:

- To set up as a **charitable association** (Statute d'Association Loi 1901). This has been tried as a scam to avoid tax, perhaps on the assumption that charities get tax breaks, or that it is easier to deal with. Friend's experience shows it actually saves nothing because, as an employee of the association you will pay Cotisations that amount to 10% of the money you draw, weekly or monthly. Then the Association (your business) pays 100% of your wages as their contributions for you, and if any profits remain in the business at the end of the year then you have all manner of difficulties justifying taking the profits without (I understand) declaring them as wages.

- To set up a simple **UK company** that declares profits in England. This is a common scam, one that is seen as an obvious way around the rules (we are in Europe, after all). It is well known to the authorities. There are strict rules for the ways in which this can be practiced, and the consequences for getting caught not abiding by the rules can be serious. You will, at the very least, have to pay all your contributions, tax in France as you should, and often you will have paid tax in the UK too! The simple rule is that, irrespective of your nationality, income should be declared, and tax paid, in the country where money is earned, or the work is done. There is a quirk, that we will explain later, that may be of interest to some.

- **Working unofficially**, otherwise known as working 'on the black'. Because of the high level of cotisations, this is a seemingly attractive option for avoiding them, as well as VAT, tax, insurance and a range of business costs. It is estimated that 30% of the French economy works on the black, so lots of people do dabble in the black economy. Oddly, many contracts 'on the black' are actually more expensive for English clients than normal contracts, perhaps just mentioning the magic words 'for cash' makes clients think it must be cheaper – often not the case. It is difficult to work entirely on the black; the English are very visible as a group and have been known to exploit the system. It is getting more common to be caught in which case the costs to the worker can be high, and the client also may face additional costs that will make the worker 'persona non grata' in the local community.

REGISTRATION

(with the 'Centre de Formalités des Entreprises', CFE)

The CFE (initials make life so much easier) is a single co-ordinating organization, working through the 'business overseeing bodies' that receives and processes business registration application forms and documents. They also oversee details on changes to, or the closing of businesses. There is a CFE office/counter in every overseeing body, such as the 'Chambre de Commerce' or 'Chambre de Métiers et de l'Artisan' (being the two most common and most well known). These bodies are similar to the Chamber of Commerce and Federation of Small Businesses in the UK, but are much more important and central to business in France than UK. Where to register depends on the nature of the business being started.

BUSINESS ORGANISATION OVERSEEING BODIES

Everyone in business needs to be registered, and the place to go for registration is the appropriate trade association for what you want to do, each grouping that in effect has much more of a central and organizing role in the business world than it does in England.

- **Chambre de Commerce et d'Industrie**:
  - Shopkeepers, no matter what you sell.
  - Commercial companies with no "artisanal" or technically skilled component to the business, where you would use the term 'sell' or 'commerce' to describe what you do. B&B establishments would be here, as well as shops and market traders.

- **Chambre de Métiers et de l'Artisan**:
  - Tradespeople, artisans such as builders, carpenters, cooks, hairdressers, indeed anyone where you could be seem to have a craft, and that includes many professions.
  - Companies combining craft and commerce.

- **Chambre Nationale de la Batellerie Artisanale**:
  - Sole traders and companies involved in inland water transportation.

- **Greffe du Tribunal de Commerce**:
  - Non-trading companies and companies with a non-commercial purpose.

- Industrial and publicly-owned commercial establishments (EPIC).
- Companies of regulated professionals.
- Commercial agents, in all fields of commerce we understand from musical, instruments to houses!

- **URSSAF**, who act to collect social contributions, and act as overseers of employment law:
    - Regulated and non-regulated professionals, such as architects and journalists,
    - Employers whose company is not registered with the commercial or trade authorities.
    - People engaged in casual work of all sorts, from child care to gardening.

- **Service des Impôts des Entreprises**:
    - Artists and writers who are often excused cotisations.
    - Other activities not fitting the above groups (such as people whose main income comes from the rental of property).

- **Chambre d'Agriculture**:
    - Individuals and companies operating in agricultural activities, especially important for those who buy land over 10 hectares, where you are expected to use the land profitably.

Finding your appropriate centre is not too difficult. You could look via the Internet, or do as many others do, by going along to your local 'Chambre de Commerce' and asking. You are likely to be helped by someone who has at least some English. If you get into a fix with the language, or if you overstep the mark, be polite and plead ignorance. Experience shows that they may register you at the Chambre de Commerce anyway.

One of the problems here in France is the number of departments that seem to multiply every time you look. Do not worry, the majority of people who trade on the high street or buy things to re-sell will register with the Chambre de Commerce, and skilled people with the Chambre de Métiers as it is known in its shortened form. Most other people will be referred to URSSAF as everyone knows it.

Let's get back to the formalities of starting and registering your business. The CFE distributes each element of a business registration application to the respective government departments for processing:

- **INSEE**, which registers the company with the Répertoire National des Entreprises (RNE) and allocates a SIREN number, a SIRET number and the APE number. These numbers are very important and identify the company, and are used to prove legality. This becomes your identity.
- **Tax services.**
- **Social security services (URSSAF).**
- The **Greffe du Tribunal de Commerce** if the activity is commercial.
- The **Répertoire des Métiers** if the activity is a trade or the person an artisan.
- The **Caisses Socials and Inspection du Travail** if there are to be employees at the start of trade. The Caisse Social is much like the social services in practice. This section is the one where you can have greatest difficulty when times get tough.

IMPORTANT NUMBERS TO REMEMBER

There are several numbers that relate to working in France. The most common is the SIRET number, but each has its part to play.

The SIRET number

The SIRET number identifies the business. This number is quoted in all dealings with local social services, tax offices and ASSEDIC (the benefits office), as well as being on all official company letters, invoices and quotations. It is the one number that you need to have. The SIRET is a 14 digit number consisting of the 9 digit SIREN number with an additional 5 digits code added.

The SIREN number

The SIREN number is made up of three groups of three digits, and is the business reference number used by French administrative offices.

Examples of SIREN and related numbers and letters (just for interest and clarity):

- For Commercial individuals and companies:

    RCS PARIS 123 456 789

    where 'RCS' is the company and trade register, 'PARIS' is the place of registration, and '123 456 789' is your Siren number

- For Artisans and trades:

    123 456 789 RM 987

    where '123 456 789' is your Siren number, RM is the register of the trades, and '987' is the number identifying the chamber where you registered

The SIREN number is not often used, except perhaps by your accountant, but a subset of it is vital. This is the SIRET number, and is the most important number you are expected to quote on all company letters and documents. It follows you everywhere!

The NAF code

The NAF code identifies the stated primary activity of the business at the time of registration. The French do like to put people and businesses into boxes, and each 'box' or business classification is numbered, which is the NAF code. The trick, when your business is described and registered, is to put in place those activities that you may *want* to do in the future. The French system finds it most difficult to deal with broad definitions of what you do, and to work in a specific area you must have the NAF code that allows you carry out that work. So, in the building trade, a draughtsman will have a different code to a roofer or electrician. If you want to work across a number of disciplines, you would do well to specify these as you start, or describe your interests in a more general category.

We have run across situations where a couple have registered a B&B business, and believed this entitled them to do a few other 'bits' on the side. The husband got very involved in the building trades, but was informed that he was 'not registered'. He could have got into serious trouble, no matter that he declared his income! However the French are only people, and people everywhere make (and understand) mistakes. Perhaps the secret is to not worry too much about minor infringements, but declare anything that comes close to a full time (or even significant) interest. Of course, we have found that shrugging and saying sorry, you didn't understand, goes a long way to making people feel better – if you are believable. As with anything official, rules are rules and if you break them it is down to you.

The TVA number

The TVA number (VAT by another name) is issued to companies and individuals providing services or selling goods and products. Registration is obligatory above a certain threshold of income, optional below that threshold. We were informed that registration was necessary over around an annual turnover of €76,300 at the time of writing (check this for yourselves), but confusion exists as to when you reach this! It seems from experience very unclear from anywhere as to when this applies! We have been informed from officials and accountants that you should register for TVA if you meet any of the following criteria:

- Your annual turnover in the previous year was 'over the threshold'.
- Your monthly turnover goes past 1/12 of the annual threshold.
- You expect your annual turnover to exceed the limit this year.
- Your quarterly turnover goes past ¼ of the annual threshold.

Perhaps the best advice is to speak to an accountant. If you reach the threshold for TVA, your business should be using an accountant by then and the accountant will know best how to deal with your particular situation.

You should consider TVA carefully, it has pros and cons. The entry level for TVA is very low, and at 19.6% TVA rate for the majority of businesses can add significantly to what you must charge. Many people like to stay away from TVA, for as long as possible. You may feel that slightly lower prices than your competitors, but no TVA, gives you an advantage in price and a much better profit margin! There will however always come a time when you can no longer avoid registration. A TVA number must be quoted on all invoices issued by a TVA-registered business.

NAMES AND LOGOS

The only way to protect a business name and/or logo in France is to register it as a trademark (*dépôt de marque*). This requires making an application, completing a form and paying a fee with INPI, details can be found at www.inpi.fr, or at your local Chambre de Commerce or Chambre des Métiers. The concept common in England of "prior use", does not exist in France (we have been told) so if you have used an unregistered name or logo, then that can carry no legal weight. However, except in extreme and unusual circumstances this will not become an issue, and you should be able to sort out any problems (especially if you have prior ownership of an internet domain name).

ENTREPRISE INDIVIDUELLE (a sole trader) or MICRO ENTREPRISE

The 'Entreprise Individuelle' (literally a business run by an individual) is used to operate as a self-employed person in just about any area of work.

Start-up costs are low, it is easy to start, and the process takes relatively little time. Many start as an Entreprise Individuelle, a 'Micro Entreprise'. In this form, the operator and their business are treated as one, but you have unlimited liability if things go wrong, which means that you are personally liable for company debts. So a spouse may also be liable to repayment of any debts, and has to sign to say they understand this. However at the point of starting (but not after), it is possible to isolate and protect your home from any business failure, get more advice about this from a notaire.

People registering in this way do not officially take on a business or trading name – they trade under their own name as far as the authorities go. You can choose a commercial name in addition, as long as there is no trademark protection already on that name. If you do have a trading name, and you adopt it from the start, be careful that you do not choose a name that will limit you should your business really work. For example, 'Joe Little, odd job plumber' on every advert is likely to limit both the size and type of job you get, and if you do grow, you will probably want to change your business name. 'JL International SARL, Plumbers to the Stars' may be a touch grand for rural France, but there are many options in between! Trading names should be carefully chosen.

Process to set up the operation

The documents required by the CFE (remember the 'Centre de Formalités des Entreprises' – spoken about earlier) can vary depending on the activity you plan, but will include the following:

- An application for registration (*demande d'immatriculation*). These may be specific to the operation being started which you will get from them.

- Proof of your address (a recent electricity bill from EDF will do), quite often this is requested as a form of proof.

- Proof of identity, for example your passport.

- Proof of your ability to trade in that business (qualifications or attestations of experience).

- Your spouse must provide written proof that they have been told and understand the consequences of debt. This is a signed form.

83

Going along to your local 'Chambres' will make this easier to understand. Submit the documents to the appropriate local CFE desk in the 'Chambre', processing time is generally two to ten days at which point the business is officially open for trade. Practically, once the forms are submitted, you're off and running!

A spouse or registered partner may help with the business on a regular basis but their role should be declared to the CFE. They will be assigned the role of collaborator (*collaborateur* – but it does not have the 'Allo Allo' connotations enjoyed by the English), employee (*salarié* if they are paid a salary, very unlikely) or associate (*associé*). In reality, helping out by keeping the books or answering the phone gets forgotten about. Many partners add support that way! Like many situations, odd details get forgotten about and anyway, times change.

THE STAGE

As a new entry to the business community you will be expected to undertake a 'stage' (the 'a' pronounced in the same way as 'sarge' when referring to the army rank). It introduces you to the process you must undertake, and many of the business rules and ideas you should know. It is full of advice, and that way the authorities have been seen to assist you, therefore it must be your fault if you get things wrong or the business fails!

Unfortunately few courses are in English. If you are expected to do this in French, and even if you are of reasonable fluency, the benefits you will get are minimal, I am informed! One friend said that he would have had more benefit from sitting at the back and reading a newspaper! However, this course can be beneficial, and there are places where it is run for people like you, who speak English. The Chambre des Métiers in Dinan run the course in English, and are very helpful.

TAX AND THE SMALL BUSINESS

A major benefit for a Micro Entreprise is that you do not need to submit annual books for audit although like any business, your accounts may be checked at any time by tax authorities.

A big benefit of being a sole trader is that accounting is supposed to be as simple as possible, and you may not even need an accountant. The system is simple, although the exact numbers may change from time to time. It works in this fashion. You sell your services, for example, and have money that comes into the business. After you deduct the costs of materials you have had to buy, to sell on for specific jobs, you are left with what is effectively your income. It is assumed that around 52% of the business (your) income goes out on expenses (phone, office, printing, transport and mileage etc), which leaves you 48% as profit. Half of this profit is charged as cotisations or your contributions, and you get to keep the rest, which you declare for income tax. It really is straightforward.

As an example, let us imagine your business turns over €35,000 in the year. €15,000 is material you buy to do the work you do, leaving you €20,000 income. Of this they accept that 52 % (€10,400) goes on running your business, leaving you €9,600 as pure taxable profit. Cotisations will be around 50% of this. However, if you keep your business costs down, anything you save will effectively be a tax free bonus to you. If you don't spend 52% on running your business, the money you save goes in your pocket. It pays to be thrifty!

The current limits for being a Micro Entreprise as laid out are; annual turnover of €27,000 for 'services', excluding any TVA, and €76,300 if you buy goods to re-sell. Beyond this and you should become incorporated. It may seem unnecessary at one level, yet at another it is good protection, and can save you money. There are always those that somehow get around the system, and just recently I heard of one builder who had not incorporated, had turnover seriously in excess of this, only to lose control and become insolvent (unable to pay his bills). It has wrecked his life, with house and all possessions being sold.

A LIMITED COMPANY, EURL or SARL

This is as close as France comes to a simple limited company as you find it in England, and something you will probably already understand. You have capital invested in the business, have shares of that capital and, as the owner of the business, your liability if things go wrong is limited to the money you have invested in the business. The business has its own separate legal identity, separate to you, and although you may own the business, even work in and control the business, ultimately your liability if things go wrong is limited.

With a **EURL**, the business is wholly owned by a single individual and is a limited liability single shareholder corporation. One person owns the company. In the case of a **SARL**, the business can have a minimum of two and maximum of 100 partners. Neither of these is quoted on the stock exchange, they are both private companies.

In both the EURL and SARL the company can be established with any amount of capital from €1. Clearly, as you have to declare your share capital, if you start with €1, about 80p at today's rate, this does not give the impression of a company set upon sturdy foundations. The bigger the capital base, the more secure the company, but the more you risk losing if things go wrong. In reality, many companies are formed with little capital, other than the value of the equipment you use in the business.

Setup process

The whole process of setting up a company in England is easy, and not expensive. Indeed, you can buy 'off the shelf' companies and be in business immediately. In France the process is much more time consuming, is in complex legal French, and while it is possible to do it yourself, it is seriously easier to use an accountant to help. You will need a good accountant anyway, both for the annual accounts and the huge amounts of official mail you will receive.

Several of the issues that need to be dealt with include the statutes and articles of association (make these as general as you can, for future flexibility), establishing an official business address, and publishing a notice of company formation in an appropriate publication. The accountant can easier deal with the CFE and provide full documents, and when all documents have been properly submitted, the business is open for trade.

Tax and accounting is complex for companies in France, as are the volumes of official mail, and the advice of a professional accountant is worth the expense. The role of the accountant in France is different than in England. They are there, or so it seems, to ensure that the company books are properly declared, whereas in England an accountant sees his or her role as minimizing your tax bill! It is an unusual accountant in France that takes this 'client-centred' approach. Therefore, if you wish to minimize your tax bill, either build a good relationship with your accountant, or take an interest to find avenues to reduce tax!

Running a limited company is, in practice, no different from running a Micro Entreprise, you just need to be more thorough in keeping records and accounts. It is no more difficult, and indeed, starting a small business is a good lead into running a much larger operation. If there is a concern, you will probably find it difficult growing your business and doing the work, until you get to the point where your business is big enough to afford you just to manage and run your business affairs.

A WAY AROUND COTISATIONS?

People in business in France rightly see cotisations as the biggest problem they face. Expected to be paid throughout the year, in an EURL or a SARL, an employee pays 10% of their salary, and the company contribution is to match their salary (in addition to the wages) paid to the country's coffers. Then, just to make it all even more complex, if you decide to take a low salary to help the company grow, the profits that the company earns are charged for cotisations too, so you will still be caught.

There are two issues associated with this, first, the salary you draw, and second, the profits that the company makes. So, if you draw no salary, then obviously you pay no cotisations. Also, if your company pays all its profits to a parent company in England (for example), then while it pays corporation tax locally, it does not pay cotisations because the profit does not go to an individual!

So a way around cotisations could be to have an English or other EU company, which sets up a subsidiary here in France. All the trade is done through the subsidiary, and everything is 100% legal, but you draw no salary, and live on the previous year's profits paid to you after they have passed everything through your UK company's accounts and Companies House! You pay no UK tax because all of your profits and your business operations were done outside of the UK. You can take some money from the business in mileage and rental of business premises.

For the English resident who does not want to work all the time, this is a good way to organize your affairs, as it allows you the flexibility to work legally as and when you wish, without the need to pay 'social charges' all year, at a prescribed time.

One downside of paying no cotisations is that you are not contributing to the social costs, so are not entitled to use the health or social systems. The way most find around this is to pay themselves the minimum wage for three months, costing cotisations of around €1,200. Small price to pay for the benefits that it brings! The other downside of setting this system up is the cost, which at current rates can vary between €1,000 and €2,000. This system is legal, well known to the social services, and is used by large numbers of registered French companies who otherwise would not be able to stay in business. Speak to your accountant.

CHEQUE EMPLOI SERVICE (CESU)

Finally comes the issue of Casual Employment. Working for cash is illegal in France, despite the large amount that everyone says exists, but casual work can be done officially, and the system itself recognizes the need for flexibility when it comes to small jobs. The CESU (as it is sometimes called) system exists to effectively allow people who do small, part time jobs for private householders (or similar) on an almost casual basis, without complex accounting systems, and the workers still pay their social and other contributions. It is an easy way to ease yourself into the world of work, and start a business in France – although almost by definition you will be working at something that (without you change the scale of work you do) is unlikely to make you a fortune.

Effectively your client acts as an employer and you as the employee, so a major benefit of this comes in the form of effective self-employment with worker protection! By paying with the 'cheque d'emploi', all administration is done automatically. Using the Cheque d'Emploi means that both client and worker are acting legally, automatically insured for accident in the home as well as being eligible for tax rebates (the employer) and social security (the employee) benefits. Typically someone using this scheme will work for a number of people who you use your services often, and on a regular if infrequent basis. It is also a low cost way for people to get domestic and household help, as the costs are low, so the charges do not need to be as high as with someone working for themselves!

To enter the system an employer (really your client) must first register with their local branch of URSSAF in the Chèque Emploi Service department. This can also be done via an application at the bank that manages their account. Payment is made to you using a pre-printed URSSAF cheque and sent to the CESU department using the pre-addressed envelope. They work out the contributions, and send a legally required pay slip to you. You get paid, and they do all the paperwork!

The advantages to your clients include:

- They are automatically fulfilling the legal obligations to pay social charges.
- Insurance is there should you have an accident while at work.
- Your clients benefit from a tax reduction of 50 percent of the amount paid to you, although for child care, this amount is 25 percent. Still, it does make it easy to employ people around the home!

The advantages to you:

- You receive the same social rights that apply to any employed person – quite significant – while having the freedom of self employment.
- You are insured in the event an accident at work.
- You can prove your social security contributions (which allows for supplementary pension and unemployment insurance).
- You get access to vocational training funded by Assedic, which can be quite significant if you want to improve your skills or start something else later.

Jobs that can be on the scheme include all domestic work, small scale gardening, child minding, home helps, odd repair jobs and maintenance, and any help to mothers with young children. It is possible that work associated with the ill or elderly can also be accepted under the scheme, such as meals on wheels and providing transport for shopping etc. The employer/your client should provide the tools necessary to do the job.

STATUTE D'ASSOCIATION LOI 1901

When you arrive in France, in your commune you will find many of the activities and associations are run as a charitable event which either draws commune money or feeds money to local 'good causes'. These forms of organization are not applicable for businesses, although some (wrongly) see them as a scam to avoid tax ... then promptly get burned.

If however you want to start an activity with the benefits going to a good cause (a cause other than your bank account), such as raising funds to pay for the local church bell restoration, this may be applicable. When you are talking this through with people locally, advise your Mairie of what you plan, and they will both guide and help you to set this up.

5

Your finances

"When you realise you've made a mistake, take immediate steps to correct it. Better still; don't make it in the first place!"

In this section we will be looking at the finances that will be important to you in business. We will not be dealing with complicated issues, and will help you to understand the ideas behind business finance that you can apply to your own situation.

When you go into business, finance is not uppermost on your mind. You will want to concentrate on what you do, and give priority to the practical issues you face, but having a background understanding of business finances helps, and will make you more successful.

For the issues associated with forecasting, and to help you with business planning, some sample forms and spreadsheets can be downloaded at www.OldKingCole.co.uk. The formats are simple – you fill in the appropriate boxes, and the computer works out all your forecasts for you!

BREAKEVEN SALES

This simple idea shows you how much you need to sell in your business to cover your costs. Knowing this also helps you to get the most from your business by focusing on the changes necessary to improve your profitability.

Just 'breaking even' means that your company does not make a profit or a loss. Making a profit means your sales are above breakeven, therefore making a loss means your sales must be below breakeven.

To explain how to calculate breakeven, it is easiest to use a simple example. We must however use some simple, almost self-explanatory terms.

- **Variable costs** – these are the costs that vary directly (well just about directly) with the level of sales, and are sometimes known as direct costs. There are only really a limited number of variable costs, and these are the costs of things you buy to resell or materials to make things you later sell, any labour costs associated with making things to sell, and delivery costs sending things sold to your client. Any administration costs, or time spent on other things does not apply here. Variable costs can be traced back to the objects you sell – entirely.

- **Fixed costs** – the costs that stay about the same whether sales go up or down, are not directly linked to specific products or clients. These are also known as expenses or indirect costs. For example, rental costs, general expenses, telephone and administrative costs, taxes and costs of things that do not vary whatever level of activity you have are included here.

- **Gross Margin** – Gross margin, a variation of the gross profit, is the difference between the value of sales and how much those sales have cost you directly, then expressed as a percentage of sales. The Gross Profit, your sale less variable costs, is shown as a Euro or Pound value or then as a percentage of sales to find the Gross Margin. The reason we prefer the term Gross Margin instead of Gross Profit is simply for clarity. At the end of the day it really does not matter what you call something as long as you understand what you mean! As a guide, your Gross Margin should be in excess of 40%, if it is less, then your direct costs are too high, and you should find cheaper suppliers, or increase your sales or charges.

- **Net Profit** – this is the profit that remains (hopefully) when you have paid for all your expenses, and is the profit that your business is taxed upon. As a guide this should be over 10%. Some people find it perhaps immoral to make a profit, but if you take the money that you have invested in your business, and just leave it in the bank, you can get around 5% return without any risk! If you do make 10% net profit, remember that you will be taxed on it, so this size of profit is not much. Riskier businesses should expect more.

Before you can work out your breakeven, you need to find your Gross Margin and your fixed costs. I'll use a few numbers here in an example to help explain how things work. It is easier then, and explains itself. Imagine your business has numbers that look like this:

Sales	**€50,000**	
Variable Costs	**€30,000**	**(direct labour, purchases & transport)**
Gross Profit	**€20,000**	**(50,000 – 30,000)**
Gross Margin	**= Gross Profit/Sales**	
	= 20,000/50,000	
	= 40%	

In this example the Gross Margin is 40%.

What are *your* fixed costs, or what do you think they will be (if you do not know exactly, have a good guess)? Only you will know. They may include …

- Costs such as advertising, marketing and promotions.
- Sales costs including salaries and cotisations.
- Renting premises and costs like electricity and rates.

- Interest on loans to improve premises in fact the interest on any business loan.
- The costs of computers and other equipment.
- Admin charges (accountant and any legal or trade subscriptions or costs).
- Memberships and other professional association charges.
- General transport and company cars.
- Other annual costs you have in the business.
- Your wages.

Assume your fixed costs in this example total €16,000 (providing a Net Profit of €20,000 – €16,000 = €4,000).

Your **breakeven sales** (the sales you need to break even) can now be calculated by dividing your fixed costs by the Gross Margin.

With fixed costs of €16,000 and a Gross Margin of 40%, the breakeven point will be €16,000/40% = €40,000.

It is important to realise that we are dividing the fixed costs by the Gross Margin, a percentage, and this can sometimes be confusing. 40% is actually 40/100, which calculates to be 0.4. So if you divide 16,000 by 0.4, you find that the answer comes easily. Care is needed here, but you have the example to help you! What does this tell you?

Here, in this example, you have to sell €40,000 of goods just to break even.

With sales of €50,000, you only make your profit on the last €10,000!

So how can you use this information? Well, to improve of course. Obviously you can increase your sales, but this does not necessarily mean more profit as you could increase costs, and sometimes your costs increase disproportionately. If you increase sales, you may actually make less profit!

It does not pay to always sell more and more,
sometimes you can make more profit by selling less!

But there are certainly routes to take. By knowing your breakeven point highlights where the problems could be, and the action that you *could* take.

It is great to improve sales if your breakeven sales point stays the same, but as you increase sales your costs may well increase – more staff, more cars or vans, costs of borrowing go up, as may storage costs (at least costs may go up in the short term and leave you dangerously short of cash – known as 'overtrading'). So be careful.

You could reduce your variable costs by finding cheaper sources of supply, or control costs better (try even not incurring some of these costs in the first place ... like unnecessary visits to clients, or too much time spent making things), thus decreasing Gross Profit.

Fixed Costs could be reduced – often not quite as easy as it sounds, as these are long term costs such as finance costs or services that you feel are indispensible.

When you know your business, and your breakeven sales, you are certainly in a much better position to make decisions on how to improve. Again, lets again use a simple example to show what could be possible.

In the example we have used, imagine that you are not happy with your overall situation, and feel the need to make improvements. What could be done, and what effect would that have? Well, the position could perhaps be improved, you decide, by small improvements that result in (say) variable and fixed costs both being reduced by 5 %. Variable costs therefore are now reduced to €28,500 (from €30,000), and fixed costs to €15,200 (from €16,000). How will this impact your finances and positively impact your business?

Your Gross Profit is:	**€21,500**	**(€50,000 – €28,500)**
Your Gross Margin is:	**43%**	**(€21,500/ €50,000 as a %)**
Your Breakeven is:	**€35,350**	**(€15,200/43%)**

Small improvements in cost mean you can get by with a major reduction in sales, and still make a profit. If you keep your sales the same and reduce costs, by just a small amount, profit rises significantly. It could make the difference between your success and failure!

You will understand that you will not be in line for a profit until your whole year's fixed costs are covered.

CALCULATING HOURLY RATES

Many people use breakeven point to understand what they need to charge for every hour of their time, to enable them to earn a reasonable living from the time they spend working for a client. Calculating hourly rates is quite easy, especially for people who keep invoices in two components – a charge for labour and a separate charge for materials.

This is because the materials vary according to the jobs you work on, and the hourly rate covers your fixed costs and any substantial areas of profit.

A generally accepted base for the number of hours that you will work in a year is 1,600. This is based upon allowing time for selling and organising materials, holidays and bank holidays, weekends off (although you may wish to work weekends), and necessary administration.

Let's assume you are a plumber with fixed costs of €16,000 per year. This is the minimum that must be earned to cover your fixed costs. Any money for you is on top of this! So working on the example given, and knowing that people will usually work 1,600 hours per year, this means that the hourly rate is €10 per hour just to cover fixed costs. Anything for you must be in excess of this.

Just to cover costs you need to earn €16,000/1,600 hr = €10/hr

If you want to earn a living, you must charge an extra amount to pay you for your time. This can be calculated in the same way.

Let's assume you want to earn €16,000 every year, then (as you only have 1,600 hours to earn it), you have to charge an extra €10 per hour. It is just common sense, really.

So, you have to charge €20 per hour (€10 + €10), just to earn €16,000 per year.

So your hourly rate can easily be adjusted depending upon what you expect to earn. You know that you have to earn €10 per hour just to cover costs, so the more you want to earn, the more you need to charge per hour. The difficulty is that the more you charge, the less hours you may be asked to work.

However, you need to understand that here in France, if you earn €10 per hour, you will lose some of what you charge as your variable costs (transport to work, meals at lunchtime if you are away from home and other general bits and pieces), and the government will take around 50% of your cut as cotisations. Looking therefore at €10 per hour for you, you will be lucky to keep around €3 per hour, which for many is unacceptable. So you increase your charges to compensate, and charge €30 per hour, perhaps more. The trouble then becomes, while you only earn a reasonable living, clients think you must be earning a fortune!

The figures chosen have quite a resonance with real life in rural France, and one of the causes of friction between artisans and clients who are unaware of the range of business costs. Typically the costs given as fixed costs are not out of order, especially if you need to buy tools and equipment, plus buy and run a vehicle. You will be able to see that even charging €10 per hour you will not earn a living, so hourly rates really start at €25 per hour of which €10 (about) is for fixed costs, and just a small proportion for you! Typical charges for good experienced tradesmen typically are up to €35 per hour in rural areas, perhaps more in large cities. And remember, profit is on top of what you take out of the business as your wages.

Working 'on the black' generally still works out at around €20 per hour as a minimum, no matter you are not paying cotisations, you still have a limited number of hours, you still have fixed costs, and you still have to get to the job – so you still have variable costs!

CASH FLOW

A cash flow forecast is, quite simply, a record of when you think you will receive money into your business ... and when you think you will have to pay it out.

'Cash is King' is a well known phrase, and no matter how good your business, the amount of money you have at any one time to pay your bills is vital. Cash is really access to money at short notice, and could include 'cash', agreed overdrafts, and loans agreed at the bank but not yet used. If you cannot pay your bills, your creditors (those people you owe money to) will not really care how profitable you are, they will want to be paid simply because their business depends upon you paying.

So, when you are planning, yes you will know what you hope to sell, you need to make realistic assumptions of when you will receive cash, and when you will pay it out. The purpose is to find when your *need* for cash is at its greatest, and you can decide how you will overcome any problems you may see coming!

Sales and money from clients are the main flow of cash into the business, and you should know in general terms at least when you can expect the money to come to you. You may accept cash over the counter, and then there is no problem. However, you may do project work, and be paid at certain stages of the work with some held for a period after you have finished. Or you may sell to shops who demand 'cash or return' terms to ease their cash flow problems, in which case things may not be sold for months. Or you may give some time as credit before payment, so from the moment the goods are delivered you may have to wait months to be paid!

Beware, everybody wants to hang onto cash, especially businesses, and there are many ways in which companies can delay payments. One trick for small businesses, especially working on contracts, is to ask for a certain percentage of the ultimate cost as a deposit upon acceptance of terms, which at least covers the costs of any materials you have to purchase. Try to include in your terms that failure to pay on time could result in increased costs. If they moan at this you can assume they will be poor payers!

'Cash out' is for everything you spend, and quite often this can go out frighteningly quickly! It often helps if you can get certain items where you pay after you have received the goods, i.e. you have them on credit. Typically creditors are suppliers, large corporations and banks, and the state.

Your cash flow forecast, is simply a look at sales, and a breakdown of costs and when they will be paid. To this you include what your fixed costs or expenses will be, and when these will be paid. You know the money you start with in the bank account, and adjust this month by month, adding money in from sales, and subtracting money that you have paid out – including your wages. So, month by month you will know how much money you should have left in the bank.

Any stock, as well as unused equipment, is dead money sitting there – so keep it to a minimum. Despite the temptation, you really do have to control this, it is absolutely key – especially in a world where the pace of change is growing. To make things for stock is becoming dangerous in even traditional industries. If you make things to re-sell, to build common components in advance can increase efficiency in some respects, but as customisation and choice is becoming the norm, to return to the philosophy of Henry Ford (where you could have any colour as long as it was black) is madness. So know what your stock is, against specific orders if they are large enough, but at least keep a track of what money is lying around dormant.

Your aim is to ensure that the right amount of cash is in the right place at the right time. Everybody is in the same position, in France as in England. There are a number of ways you can improve your position, especially valid if you are dealing with English clients that have holiday homes in France, and who may not want to pay until they have seen the quality of finish. These are common sense.

- Ensure customers know your terms and conditions, and ask for a deposit to at least cover any materials needed. That way you will not be out of pocket except for your time.

- Do not forget to send invoices – ask to be paid – and get the details right.

- Do not be embarrassed to ask to be paid.

- Be careful of key dates and watch when invoices are paid. In France you can be penalised for late payment!

- If you are promised a cheque, follow it up. A cheque in France has the same value as cash, as it is illegal to not have the funds to cover any cheque written.

- Keep records of outstanding credit, and notes of what any particular customer has had in terms of goods or time but have not yet paid for.

I can only remember one occasion when a client had disputed a bill, and found that records of cost and time were invaluable. It became clear that payment would not be forthcoming, so rather than get involved in a major fight, and spend valuable time in fruitless argument, it became obvious that I would need to evaluate what had been purchased for them, then go back to their property and remove it, to the approximate value to what had been lost. It is always unsavoury, but there comes a time when you have to cut losses and write off invested effort. It is sad when this happens, everybody loses, but at least everyone shares the pain. Was it legal? Who knows?

The situation is though more serious where you are owed large amounts of money. You are in effect financing other people's pleasure or businesses; they are using your money to finance what they want. Poor payers are poor payers because they do not want to pay you. The longer you leave a debt, the greater the risk. The trick is not to let that kind of situation arise. Keep control of what you are owed!

PROFIT AND LOSS FORECAST

Planning your profit and loss is an important step to understand if all your big ideas about your business will end up with you making a profit at the end of the day. It sounds silly, but many good ideas actually do not, and are better left as just good ideas!

To help you in this process, a basic forecast spreadsheet can be downloaded at www.OldKingCole.co.uk. This is not fancy, and there are many examples on the market, but it does take all of the calculations away from you, makes financial planning easier. All you need to do is fill in all the self explanatory boxes.

Why is this useful? Well, looking at the way a sales forecast is laid out, you will see that it is nothing more than your anticipated income from sales, month by month. These add up to your total income. From this we will see all of your direct or variable costs, things you buy to re-sell, labour costs and distribution charges. Taking one from the other you are left with your Gross Profit, and can easily calculate you Gross Margin! You are nearly there!

Now you can add up all of your fixed costs or general expenses, and you can take them from your Gross Profit to leave you a Net Profit. This is the profit that you are in business for. This builds up month by month until you have a picture of what your year will look like (financially) if everything goes to plan. You will see if the profit you plan is enough, and gives you the opportunity to change things if they are not good enough! It lets you play with your plans and judge how good they are.

Once you start, month by month, your fixed costs will be fairly standard, can be budgeted, and the only areas where you can influence profits are in the volume, value and cost of sales. Knowing what options are open to you from the section on Breakeven, you will be able to look at your plans quite objectively, and it is good to play with different options before you start. It is far better to spend time playing with options before you start than when you realise you are having problems.

Having planned for a year or two ahead, you can refer back to this forecast regularly and see how well you are doing compared to your plan. This lets you see at an early stage whether you will achieve the results you forecast, and because it is timely, lets you plan improvements should you need to, while you are still in a position to influence the outcome.

KEEPING CONTROL

Computers make it easy to keep a record of how the business is doing, storing data in whatever form is as simple as pushing a button. Therein is a problem. Why are you keeping all this information, and what are you going to do with it?

Computers let you manipulate all kinds of information, but having all that information locked away on disc makes it unlikely that it will ever be used, and looking at numbers makes it hard to see trends. If you want to keep records, and let this information help you into the future, perhaps the best way to do it is using graphs. You can choose those figures that have meaning, and put them in pictorial form so that you can see trends.

What sort of information could you consider useful? Well, that depends upon you. Sales, Gross Profit, Net Profit, are obvious candidates, but there could be more. There are examples given in the financial planning tool should you wish, that you can use. There is no point in keeping any information unless you are using this on a regular basis to improve your business.

Obviously when running a business there are some numbers you must know – a combination of certain financial information and operational information. This information needs to be looked at regularly as is needed to see if things are going well, or not. Try to see trends, as they occur!

Typically you should be looking at …

- The value of your sales, and if this is perhaps not the only indicator of good or poor performance, you could be looking at this in conjunction with customer orders (if they come to you), or just the actual number of customers who come into your shop if you have one.

- Your Gross Profit and your Gross Margin. The benefit of looking at this figure is the knowledge that this is the one area that you can easiest improve your profits. An increasing trend in sales yet poor margins, and you can do something about it.

- Your Net Profit, and Net Margin (the net profit as a % of sales) is fundamental, as this needs to be sufficient to justify being in business in the first place!

- Operational information depends upon the kind of business you have, and the number of employees if any that you have.

If you have people selling for you, the sales per person, number of visits or profit from sales could be useful. If you have employees that make things, you may look at the value and quality of things produced. If you have a restaurant, the number of serving or kitchen staff compared to the number of diners. Or perhaps you sell a range of products, and would benefit understanding how much of each line you sell. The only purpose is improvement and so the outcome of all this extra work is ... more profit.

- Then you want a plan of action, which says what you feel needs doing, and who is going to do it, by when, to improve. As time progresses, you will see the results.

COTISATIONS

As stated earlier, Cotisations, your contributions to social charges, health and pensions, are set at a percentage of individual's earnings, profit in a larger organisation, and a percentage of sales in a micro-organisation. It is vital you know what your contributions will be, and the time when you need to pay them! As you start in business, demands will be sent to you with and times when they are due.

In year 1, cotisations will be set at an affordable level, a fraction of what they could be, as nobody knows your turnover or profit. Set aside the money to pay these in full, not just what is demanded, and plan them into your finances using the cash flow forecast. In an ideal world, calculate what you should pay, speak to your accountant, and put money to one side (if possible in an interest bearing account) for the difference between what is demanded and what you should pay.

Year 2 will see an increased demand, and assumes that your business will expand. Again, calculate what you should pay, speak to your accountant, and put the extra money to one side, the difference between the two amounts. The reason becomes apparent in year 3.

Year 3 will be dreadful, so you do need to make provision for this in the early years, as this year is when the authorities regulate what you should have paid in the first years and demand their fair share of your profits from years 1 & 2. The problems that this can create are obvious, and it is not difficult to understand that in business in France, year 3 is the most difficult year you will face. The trouble is that, after a fairly lax period, the new regime is demanding. Some businesses find that no matter what they do, it is impossible to make a profit, and unfortunately some businesses close!

Accountants are very aware of the problem, and there are ways to minimize the problems created, but in years 1 & 2 it is wise to be aware that the problem exists and may arise, and budget for payments that will come. If they do not, and you have saved too much money, you have at least a pot of money to invest!

An employer's contributions are very expensive, and are approximately equal to the amount that you pay each staff member. Hence, if you pay a staff member €2,000 per month, then you must pay a further €2,000 to the state. Hence your employee costs you €4,000! For this reason, many employees are paid the legal minimum, and wages are supplemented by payments that are not considered part of salary.

Think of the consequences for your business if you employ someone. Imagine you are an electrician, busy, working 5 days a week, and charging €250 for a full day's work. Allowing for time to see clients, get materials and deal with administration, you will bring home around €1,250 for a 5 day week. However, from this you need to run your business, which costs you probably 50% of you income. Your cotisations are then 50% of the remainder, leaving you around €300 per week in your pocket. Being busy, you consider taking on staff, and you pay them the minimum wage of around €300 per week – oddly similar to you! However, this will cost you another €300 in employer's contributions, and perhaps €100 in supplementary benefits (perks), a total of around €700 per week. Then you allow for some profit for your business, reward for your risks, perhaps a further €150, and a total of €850.

To pay your new staff, you need to find more work, adequate to keep you both busy, and you have to find time from your busy week to do this. So you spend more time selling, less time doing, so your earnings go down from €1,250 to €1,000! Following the same logic as before, you need to cover your other business costs, which now may not have risen, but which surely will not have gone down.

These will still be around €600, around €500, leaving you only €400 for yourself, and you have yet to pay you cotisations, around €200 leaving €200 spare. You could be earning less than your employee, having all the risk, all the worry, and few of the perks.

As the book is being sent to the publishers, there are moves to simplify the payment of cotisations, so that new businesses can elect to pay their cotisations the month after the business was done. For some companies this will be simple to organize, and will rely both on self declaration and good regimes of book keeping. For some smaller businesses it will be good, others less so. The advice has got to be, as in all things, speak to your accountant.

This new system is known as the 'Auto Entrepreneur' and is designed to address some of the worst aspects of a heavy and bureaucratic system that draws your money from the business almost before you have made it. Because the Auto Entrepreneur system is so new, and there are incentives to take this route, many people are setting off down this road. But remember, incentives of no corporation tax are small potatoes compared to the onerous social charges or cotisations that you could face.

6

Specific financial issues

"There are some things you just can't avoid,
no matter how much you try."

INSURANCE

Like anywhere, insurance covers very many aspects in France. There is health insurance, car or vehicle insurance, home or business insurance, public liability insurance, life insurance, insurance for your inability to work, and insurance against your ability (or otherwise) to do the work you say.

The trouble with being in business is that, from time to time, no matter how conscientious you are, no matter how good your quality control, things go wrong. It need not be your fault, and your client may be very understanding, but when things go wrong they can be expensive to fix. Yes, you could find reasons for the problem, but whatever you say, and however right you are, you are already in a rearguard situation and protecting yourself against the extent of your involvement. Insurance in this situation is always a relief.

Obviously, if there are minor problems you will remedy them immediately, that is all a part of customer care, and anyone would expect you to remedy minor problems. We are not talking about apportioning blame, just looking for customer satisfaction. However, there are times when (for one reason or another) things go beyond this. Then you need professional insurance, and by law in France you must be insured for the work you do, as well as for any public liability you may have.

Naturally, the more established and the lower risk you are, the less insurance will cost you. For example, in the building trades, there is

- Minor works insurance which is good for two years but where the type on work you do is limited in size, complexity and the number of jobs you do for any one client.

- 'Decinale' insurance, good for ten years (deci is for ten, like decimal which is based on the number ten), which is required for any new buildings and major works. Obviously this is longer term, more risky, and therefore more expensive for the insurance company because there are more things that could go wrong!

It is said to be rare for new artisans (including the English setting up in business) to be able to access decinale insurance until they have been in business for three years.

Then there is the issue of professional advice, similar to the case above, where nothing tangible changes hands, but where you could be liable should things go wrong. Consultants and professionals are continually concerned about their liability, and the need for insurance will depend upon your industry and the possible consequences and costs of mistakes.

Life insurance is simply an arrangement that, should you die, you will receive some money adequate to cover certain promises to repay debts, or provide your dependants with cash to help them over the problems caused by your loss. This is the same anywhere, but when you need loans, the need for extra life insurances can significantly push up the price of borrowing. If you go to the bank for a loan, the manager will probably make the loan conditional on you taking out insurances. At one level this can be seen as a good form of protection, but then conversely, you would not be doing this if you anticipated dying!

In England there is insurance against illness or injury, and so to there is here in France! And yes, when you are taking out a loan, the bank manager will try to impress upon you the need for caution and the consequences of what may happen if you are unable to work. He (or she) will paint a picture of doom and gloom, say that you may need to sell the children or send your wife out with a begging bowl. You on the other hand will be full of optimism and confidence that nothing could happen to you! Unfortunately things do happen, and there is always a risk, no matter how slight, that the bank manager is right! It is up to you to decide whether you need this level of insurance cover, but also check how long you will need to be incapacitated before the insurance policy begins to pay out.

Public liability insurance is, in certain circumstances very important. People have accidents, or illnesses, and if you are the cause, they can claim against you. If you work away from the public, or are in a job with minimal risk, then perhaps you do not need this, but for certain groups it is mandatory. Speak to an agent, who will surely advise you have it, and make your decision based upon this and your instincts.

Buildings insurance for the home or business is essential to cover for fire and theft (the usual two) and damage from natural (or other) disasters. Your insurance costs will depend upon your circumstances and the business you are in, but if you are likely to have cash or valuable computers and equipment, then it will be tempting for any thief. Country living in France is much less risky than the UK, but this does not mean that risks do not exist, and although less prominent, drugs and the need for cash to finance bad habits exist here too.

Vehicle insurance is the same wherever you go, and is mandatory. The newer the vehicle, the more you are tempted to buy comprehensive cover to keep it looking nice whoever is to blame for the accident. In France there is less concern about the age and condition of vehicles unless this impacts the ability to work. This could impact the costs of vehicle insurance, and is for you to decide the level of insurance you need.

Health insurance is a separate issue in France to the UK, and everybody should have some kind of cover – it is the way that the system works here. Roughly put, the state insurance pays for around 65 to 70% of the costs of treatment, and you are expected to cover the rest of the cost individually or via a private insurance scheme. Even a minor trip to hospital can be expensive, even in France, and the vast majority of the population takes out at least the minimum schemes available. Because of this insurance element, all aspects of healthcare are covered and treated as you would be with BUPA in the UK, with prompt service and care. Health insurance is virtually unavoidable. It also means you are not stopped working for so long, waiting for a hospital place. Costs for insurance are not excessive, around €30 per person per month, but vary with age.

While each element of insurance is not in itself a large cost, it actually becomes very important in terms of cost when you add all the various forms of insurance together. It pays to shop around for different quotes as, with the size and complexity of the insurance market, small percentage savings can be significant. And as cost directly influences either your profit (for business insurance) or household needs, care must be taken over what you need, and how much it costs you.

VEHICLES

Vehicles could be your one big cost when setting up a business. Vans, cars and even lorries, their purchase and running costs amount to one big hit on the finances, especially with rising fuel costs. Vehicles in France are less expensive here when purchased new, or so it seems, yet second hand vehicles relatively are more expensive. This comes from the French preference to buy cheap yet sell expensive. It you need transport in France, certainly for your business, you need to consider all the costs involved – and the issues that can influence your decision on what you are going to do. This short section points out the main issues.

Second-hand vehicles here depreciate slower than in England, based a straight line basis, and depends on both age and mileage. You can find newer yet high mileage vehicles depreciated quickly, and are relatively inexpensive, and older low mileage vehicles that are seemingly very expensive for their age. Most French businesses care about reliability.

It must be up to you to choose whether to buy French, and to be frank, some are put off simply by the oddly high prices of second hand cars (marked 'Occasion'), and import a right hand drive vehicle from England, then suffer the consequences of driving on the wrong side of the vehicle.

Importing a vehicle has certain other consequences and costs. These include:

- All vehicles that are here for over a year should be re-registered in the department (region) of France where the vehicle is kept and maintained. This is true whether the vehicle comes from abroad (the UK or elsewhere) or even another department of France. There is a one-off registration cost that depends upon the size and power (puissance) of the vehicle, and its age (over 10 years old it is cut to 50%).

- The paperwork and administration associated with changing the number plate (plat d'immatriculation) is very complicated, and involves getting a certificate of mechanical conformity to French standards (the Controle Technique) that is much more stringent than the (equivalent) British MOT test. It is possible to organize the paperwork yourself, at the expense of grey hairs, much frustration and many wasted hours in queues at the regional Prefecture or departmental Sous-Prefectures. An alternative route is to ask a local garage if they will help, and on the understanding that they are going to get your future business, they will often organize the administration for you. Some may charge a small premium, but it is worth it!

- Bringing a larger vehicle, while the vehicle may be inexpensive for reasons of fuel efficiency, mileage or age, the cost for a new 'green card' can be very expensive. Small cars are significantly cheaper to register as well as run!

- Lights are always an expense, and you do need lights that dip in the right direction. Unfortunately cars from the UK have lights that dip the wrong way, and usually this is corrected by completely changing the sealed beam units, an expensive job. For older vehicles, the cost of this can exceed the UK value of the vehicle. For common French vehicles you may find replacement units at a scrap merchant, and they are easy to change if you do, but as the French tend to drive French cars (Peugeot, Renault and Citroen), less popular in England, scrap merchants tend to have many of these makes, few of foreign cars. The little temporary stick on patches that tourists have will not do!

- Servicing is another issue you should consider. Most towns have garages linked to one or more of the big French motor manufacturers. That way they have the market just about sown up. There are other main agents, but they tend to be located in big cities, and are always difficult to get to when your car breaks down! Big agents are also expensive! There are two other issues that make life difficult for 'un-French' car drivers. Modern cars are built with many computerized parts and systems, and local garages will be unable to diagnose complex faults. Then there is the question of part availability. For many models, availability of spares can be a problem, so your car or van could be sitting in a garage, unusable, for months. You then either have to borrow, hire or buy alternative transport; otherwise you are out of business.

- Finally, right-hand drive cars and vans are impossible to resell on to the French, and many long term English have already converted to 'driving on the other side' – so will not be interested in changing back.

Of course, you could do the same as some, and that is you ignore the law for as long as possible, and stay with a UK registered vehicle. Clearly that is possible to do, until you get caught, but there are several practical complications. The first is insurance. British insurers will cover you for trips to France, but not when your vehicle is effectively exported. French insurers will insure your vehicle for a while, but then will insist you change the registration to your department. Technically, if you can show that the vehicle is from the UK, has UK tax and insurance, and a UK MOT certificate if appropriate, then you can keep your UK registration and be legal. But why would you want to do that? Having done things properly and changed your number plate, gained a local registration (Carte Grise) there are no more costs than the bi-annual inspection detailed above. In trying to keep your vehicle English, you have UK tax and MOT costs, insurance premiums that may not cover you if you are caught, and possibly the aggravation of regular trips to the UK to ensure your vehicle conforms. That alone is enough to make many people change!

KEEPING ACCOUNTS

Keeping accounts in England is something that (for many in business) has all the excitement associated with insomnia. The very term 'Double Entry Book Keeping System' is enough to turn many people away from accounts. To me it is summed up by the Muppets working for Scrooge in Charles Dickens's *A Christmas Carol*. Dry, boring, with endless ledgers full of meaningless numbers. It does not have to be that way! The logic of keeping financial records is intuitive.

As a business person, you will need to know how your business is working, and will need to know your income, costs and outgoings to enable you to work out your profits. These do not need to be complicated, simple listings will do, based either on projects or on daily/weekly sales. The bigger your business, the more appropriate you find an accountant.

For normal commercial businesses, the first and classic place to start is with sales. If appropriate keep a daily or weekly record of what you have earned or sold, perhaps categorized into separate sections if it important and easy to do. This may include credit or cash sales, restaurant or bar sales, petrol or garage sales, or even tinned, frozen and fresh items if you have a grocery store – the categories are up to you. By keeping daily and weekly records you will begin to see trends and patterns of earnings or sales, and if one line does better or worse at particular times. If you have a till, keeping till records will help prove your figures if there is ever any dispute with the tax office.

You could keep your records in a book, or on separate sheets if you find it easier – it depends how complicated your business.

Generally a daily record of sales and a weekly record of costs is the most you will need. You need records, but these need to reflect your business activity.

Keep a list of your costs for things you buy in to sell. These will undoubtedly be simple to understand, for example in a shoe shop they will be the shoes, and perhaps ancillary things like polish or socks. Also keep a note of transport costs, and wages if you have staff that deal directly with what you do, deal with the customer direct. Hold onto receipts or wage slips, and keep them attached to this list. This could be important if at any future time you want to look at what your gross profit is, keeping these costs separated from the rest.

Also keep a listing of any general bills you pay, naturally with receipts, for all the other costs you have, those general business costs such as advertising, phone, rent or whatever. These are your expenses, and (when subtracted from your gross profit) let you know your profitability. Any wages you take out of the business should be listed here too, again with a note of what you took and when you took it.

Simply listing the things like this keeps it easy, you can work out your profit if you need, and is more than adequate as a record. For a Micro Entreprise you do not need to use an accountant, and simple lists like this are adequate. If you run a bigger organization, a SARL or an EARL, then giving your records to your accountant like this, together with any bank details or cheque books, is well enough organized. For larger businesses the presentation of French accounts should be done through an accountant – they know the protocols and formats for presentation. Although I understand English accounts, I'll be honest and say that the majority of accounts in France are Double Dutch – simply the layout is enough to put anybody off!

For project based businesses, in whatever industry, the way invoices (factures) are presented determines the way you can keep your records, and it is even easier than for commerce based businesses. For each client and job keep a record of what you have bought for the project, and what you have spent. Then, when you present your invoice it should be broken down into material (materiel), labour (main d'oeuvre) at an hourly rate, and total. TVA is treated separately, and added at the end. So keeping records like this will give you a gross profit, and any general costs and ancillary materials can be noted as general expenses.

The odd note is that for mileage, no matter the type of business you have, if you use your own car, you need to keep a record of where you went and when, and given the size or 'puissance' of your vehicle, you can claim so much money per kilometre. This means you have the cost of maintaining the vehicle, paying for petrol, and any associated expenses. It also means that, with care, you can make a good tax free profit from mileage, but by driving poorly, you make less. You would be surprised how much less fuel you use by driving smoother and slower! If the vehicle belongs to the business (technically), you cannot claim mileage, but can claim fuel and garage bills. If the business is VAT (TVA in France) registered, you can reclaim any VAT on the purchase of the vehicle.

Another popular way to earn 'tax free' is to charge for use of your home, if you work from home. Use of space for an office, use of the garage, whatever you use you can charge for. You have to declare this for income tax, but it lets you take money out of the company before it gets clobbered for corporate taxation ... and yes, cotisations.

7

The sales machine

"Give people more than they expect, and do it cheerfully."

All businesses need sales, even here in France. Starting a business, you will be the person most likely to be doing the selling. Even if you have a bigger business, or have someone (a partner perhaps) who will be responsible for sales, you need to know the principles of selling so that you can appreciate when things are going well or badly. Although many believe selling to be a mystical science, really it is like anything else, a process. The more you do it, the better you should be, and the more sales you will make.

Larger organisations know that the process of selling is a numbers game. Estate agency is a good example. The more properties there are in the window, the more people will look into the window and want to visit possible homes. The more visits, the more sales, and the more homes you will sell. It works, which is why estate agencies are now filled with young enthusiastic sales staff rather than more experienced people. It is the same anywhere, and to each business there will be certain keys. The more people who stop at the window of a restaurant, the more read the menu, the more will come in to eat. For a builder, the more visits to clients, the more opportunity to quote, and the more chance of work.

And what entices people to contact you? That depends, but understanding what drives your sales machine is important. That is what you must understand, influence and drive forward. Why do some people seem so good at selling? Why do some companies never seem to have any problems with getting orders, while others struggle to stay afloat from day to day? It is not that they are better people, or that they are technically better. No, they put the focus where it matters. It is not getting the orders but driving *the front end* of the sales process. It is getting the enquiries, the contacts, the visits or the introductions. The rest will follow. Selling is a numbers game.

It sounds trite, but I am about to give you a 30-second MBA. Business graduates often deal with the peripherals to business, not the essentials. They examine corporate finance, industrial relations, law and the like. My views are not meant to devalue what graduates do, only shine a light on what you must concentrate on, as a practitioner and generalist.

Business is about delighted customers. You give the customer what they want in a way that pleases them, and they are prepared to pay you the price you ask and agree.

This may all seem a bit simplistic but it is the essence of what business is all about. Happy customers are willing to pay what they see as a fair price. Notice that I did not say a low price. Well, in the vast majority of cases they are. Let your competitors deal with poor payers and people that want everything for nothing! They can be his problem. You want good customers that will value the efforts you make on their behalf, and will want to stay with you as a supplier.

So, to round off this academic gem of wisdom, how do you go about making this work? Why try to be clever? Ask customers what they want. Do not tell them what they need, nor what you can do. Ask them simply what they want. Then provide it well and at a profit. Forget the idea of a fair price for the job; make it the right price for both. Forget about low cost – when did you hear somebody judge the value of a job simply because it was cheap?

Back to the sales machine. The more people you see, the more people you talk to, the more effort you make, and the more success you will have in selling. Selling must be seen this way. If you want to sell more, drive the front end of the sales process. More sales requires more opportunity to sell. If you go to the client, fine, it requires more effort. If the customer comes to you, you just need more footfall, more people coming to you gives more opportunity to sell to them.

Again, note that I said "Sell to them" as opposed to taking their orders!

A Story

A friend of mine, in a similar field to me, tells the story of his depression when, after two years in business, things were not really working out. One evening, walking his dog he stopped and stared at a bungalow with a long drive with 'his and hers' Mercedes parked outside. He imagined they must have inherited the money or, worse but more likely, robbed someone. After all, everybody was having a tough time!

After a few minutes, it might have been ten, the owner came out and asked him what the matter was. "I'm just looking at the cars, aren't they lovely?" To which came the response, "Oh, do you want to buy one? Only I'm buying a new one myself in a few weeks. I promised myself one for my 50th, and it's my birthday soon."

This got to my friend, with his troubles. He felt it unfair until the man said, "Economic problems? I'm doing better than ever. When trade looks difficult, I just make more effort." The same will work in France, it is a numbers game, and the more effort you make, even in a poor economy, the more success you will have! It took a few days for the penny to drop for my friend, but drop it did, and he's never looked back. Everything is a numbers game, and the sales machine is just like a funnel into which you feed contacts, it has a handle you turn like a mincer, and a narrow outlet from which sales come. Feed the machine and orders will come.

The sales machine

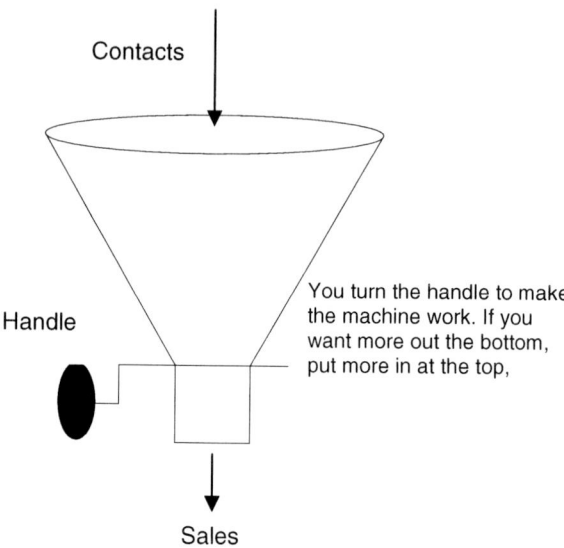

Do not try to control what comes out of the sales machine, drive what goes in. You must push the front end of the business, and if that gives you the operational problems of being too busy, then these are easier problems to deal with than not enough work! Like the estate agents who control the numbers they need to feed their machine. They control visits, estimates, and houses taken on, visits and of course sales. The rest is of no consequence to them. If one house stays on their books for ages … so what?

SELLING SKILLS IN THE SMALL BUSINESS
Selling in a small business is all about understanding the customer need, creating the impression that you can do the job, building confidence, then asking for the order.

Let's look at the sales skills of a painter and decorator. Let's say his first contact with potential customers is "I'm looking for someone to help with...". He is asked round to see the job and gives a price. Then he goes away while they make a decision. Do they choose him or the three others who are all equally able to do the same quality work. All at about the same price! Has he sold anything? Chances are that he has not.

He must be promoting himself, asking what the client is trying to achieve, give ideas, and lead the conversation so that the client really appreciates what is contributed. Also,

- **People love problems!** (Well, they love to spend time thinking and talking about them, anyway.) If you are seen to understand your customers' problems first, there will be a lot of empathy between you and customer. Link the types of problems customers may encounter to the benefits you bring.

- **People are a cynical lot.** It does not pay to give *too many* benefits, or say too much because; in the majority of cases you could be giving them a reason NOT to buy. Do not be over the top. It sounds crazy, but it's true. Know the value of knowing what *not* to say, and keep some benefits up your sleeve for later.

Everyone loves to talk, but the salesmen should know when to shut up, especially in front of clients. It is only too easy to just carry on talking, and stop listening. The salesman who says little (except to ask prompting questions and lead what is discussed) is felt to understand the problems better, know what the customer feels, be totally at one with the customer, and be in a good place to spot the benefits the client is really looking for. The customers therefore sell to themselves.

PERSONAL MOTIVATION

Personal motivation is a good driver for going out and selling. If you are hungry you will want to look for food; if you need work, you are keener to go out and sell.

I like to think of motivation like a thermometer. When it is cold we are happy to make the effort to get warm. When it is hot, few people want to do more than laze around. Most of us work to our own internal thermometer, and our effort to drive sales is usually set to this. If we are not earning enough then we make greater effort, but when we approach the top of the scale our efforts seem to slow down and we almost relax and stop. We reach a temperature where we get comfortable, and when we get comfortable … we slow down.

When you are starting in business you need to adopt a different view of money that if you are employed, almost take a 'monopoly money' approach. The money that comes in does not belong to you, it belongs to the business, and you will be lucky to keep a percentage of this. Indeed, making a good living when starting a business would be … unusual!

To replicate a salary or wage, when you're working for yourself, you need to aim for double or triple that as money coming into the business. Don't forget that when you are on holiday or out selling you are not earning. Also remember that the money that comes into the business is not all profit, and allowing for expenses and cotisations, you will spend much of what you receive. You need to set your sights high.

€ Scale

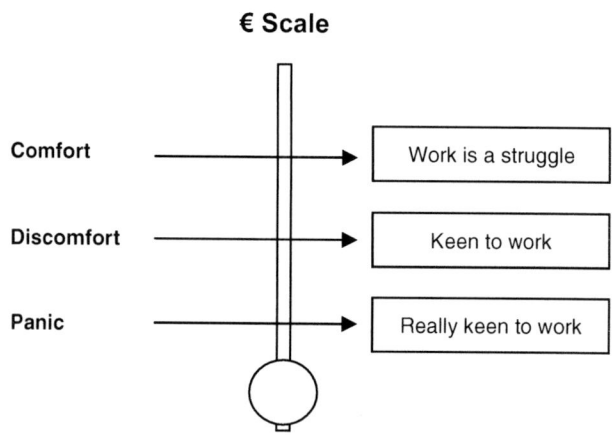

So, what does this mean to you? Perhaps, if you set your goals too low, you will be relaxed and not make the effort that you should, or perhaps you will be inclined to put off doing what you know needs to be done! Raising your own expectations and upping your game is something you need to do – perhaps if you cannot do this then you should either employ a salesman, or find a job!

Remember that temperature is relative, and what is hot for one person is not for another, so while you may have sufficient income, another earning more than you is driven for even more. There is nothing wrong with that. Equally important, money may not be your only motivator, although you need to make at least enough. There may be other things that drive you, including pride, or perhaps a desire to help others, and you need to focus on these as well to ensure that you keep driving yourself forward. It is too easy to relax.

TAKING ORDERS AND SELLING

There is a big difference between taking orders and selling. Taking an order is easy and very common, especially in shops where you would have thought they would employ sales staff. Selling is absolutely vital, but unfortunately it is an underestimated skill. There is a vast difference between taking someone's order and actually selling to them! Just because someone is called a sales assistant, and takes money in exchange for goods you buy, it doesn't mean they are actually selling anything. Mostly sales staff just wait around for your orders!

Do you recognise this? Into a shop you go, a specialist biscuit shop perhaps, armed with an amount of money and a determination to get what you feel you want. You go to the counter, ask for a bag of biscuits (for example), pay your money and go. Have they sold you anything? No. They have taken your order, met your minimum expectations and that is all. Have they sold you any cakes, or more expensive biscuits, or a loaf of bread, or even an idea that you may come in more often? Have you walked out with more than you intended to buy when you walked in? No. So they have not actually sold you anything. The closest they came to selling was when you looked into the window and were attracted into the shop.

Take the supermarkets, where there is a much more scientific approach. Go in for biscuits and you are likely to walk out with a whole bag of groceries. My wife forbids me to go shopping alone because I spend too much. Yes, we are all caught. Why? Because supermarkets actually sell, and do it best without even involving staff. Everything about a supermarket is geared to sales, organised, laid out and structured so you buy more than you anticipated when you entered. They use positioning, colours, aromas, makes, and signs – the arena of selling in supermarkets is approached as a science! They are very good at it!

So how does this impact you? Well it is simple really. You will want to get the first bite at the client's cherry, and get asked to do the first job, or give them whatever they want. However, clients have many needs, and it is likely that there is much more opportunity that waits for you. So, when you meet the client, look around, see the opportunity that could exist. Or, when you are working with a client, look and listen for more opportunity that may come your way! If they walk to your counter, talk to them, find out what they like, listen to clients over time and adapt your offerings, see each client as an opportunity – not to exploit them, but to satisfy their needs. After all, finding the client is the hardest part in making sales!

THE IMPORTANCE OF PRICE

There is a view that price is the key to selling. This is a fallacy. It is an excuse for not selling, or not having to sell. Let's be cynical again. If you employ a salesman, what's the easiest thing for him to do? He can excuse his poor sales skills by saying the price is too high or the competition is too fierce. Or he can buy work by dropping the price to the point where you make no profit ... or worse!

But what if it's you that's facing this problem, when the client wants you to drop the price? It is the natural trap when you negotiate on price. There are many ways to effectively take price out of the decision process, and that all revolves around how you make yourself different and better than the competition. Be more creative and perhaps link price to service or your high quality levels. "If you want me to lower the price, I can do that. But then that will adversely impact..." Be open and say that you price it fairly, and even ask where others will cut corners if they charge less than you!

Alas, if you are willing to lower price once, anybody in their right mind will expect similar or better discounts next time! You obviously charge too much, and have built this buffer in! You must have! Actually you have not – and by lowering your price you are just giving away your profit.

Let us consider a good example that proves the rule! If price were the main issue when it comes to buying, we'd all be driving cars at the cheapest end of the market. Who would like a Rolls Royce, or a Jaguar, or a Mercedes, or whatever? If price were the key, these cars would be very unusual. However, other factors come into play, including income, vehicle age, your age and tastes, the need for room and comfort, status symbols, what the neighbours own, indeed many factors that are completely individual. So stay away from price as a major issue, do not make it more important than it really is.

But wait a moment, not everybody is driven by service and occasionally you will find people who are set on buying for the lowest price. It is then down to you to decide if you are willing to work for nothing. There comes a time in a situation like that when you may have to admit defeat, and just walk away from the client, hard as it may be. Let someone else have him, he is a problem waiting to happen.

BEING TYPECAST

Customers do tend to associate suppliers with a limited range of goods, and put you in pigeonholes. A colleague of ours once was quite shocked when we said that we did certain jobs. "I didn't realise you do that," he said. He was soon put right! What does this mean for *you* and your sales effort? It means there could be opportunities for you that remain untapped. Your sales machine could be well fed by this alone! Look at you customers afresh. How can you set about breaking their mould?

WHAT ABOUT COMPLAINTS

Like it or not, there are times when you will not be at your best! Try to exceed expectations, but there will be times when the quality of your work does not live up to your high standards. Be careful of how you assess your own performance and if you are too willing to cut corners. Only 1 in 25 customers will complain when they have good reason, the rest moan about you to their friends, and then go elsewhere. A delighted customer will tell 10, an unhappy customer will tell 24, so it's in your interest not to have people complain – bad marketing.

So, for every complaint, you could have a bad name with potential customers. Not fair perhaps but there are things you can do about it. Every customer concern or complaint handled well usually leads to respect that you are treating them well, and probably good references and perhaps even more work. Seen in this light, a customer who is dissatisfied with your performance can be seen as an opportunity rather than a problem. But beware, you must approach the subject in a positive way, and give the impression that you really care.

TIPS

There are other tips that you may find helpful when selling to clients:

- **Anecdotes & stories**. Insurance salesmen have all got a sob story of someone who had failed to buy insurance. Car salesmen talk of people who have regretted not buying from them. In every industry and trade there is some opportunity to use the idea to advantage, and find (even embellish) stories that show how what you do has benefitted people in a very real way. It adds weight to what you say.

- **Psychology of numbers.** The number 7 is good, in my experience, and I try to build the number 7 into the price in some way. The Chinese find that the number 8 is especially fortunate. Try to understand the value that certain things add to your efforts, even if perhaps there seems no logical reason why they should. You may not understand nor agree with the theory, but if it has a positive impact then... why not try it. If it only makes you feel good, it has done its job.

- **Don't give too much choice.** Increasing the amount of choice does not make it easier for the potential client to choose; in fact it makes it harder. A simple alternative can do, if any choice is necessary, and in choosing between one option and another, they are already moving towards buying. You can slant the options to be positive. To say no then becomes so much harder.

  - "Do you want black or green?"
  - "Would you like me to deliver, or will you collect?"
  - "I'm visiting the area soon. Would you prefer this week or next?"

  And so on, there are endless variations, but once you have given then a choice, for clients to express a preference has significant consequences.

- **Use 'tie downs'.** These are simple re-affirmations after a statement to get assent. It has the impact of tying the client to you! Again they are then moving towards buying! For example:

  - "These do fit well, don't they!"
  - "This type of service is better for you/your company, isn't it!"
  - "You do feel I have understood the issues, don't you?"

  There are many variations of this technique, but with these tie downs, you are gaining small agreements which are all steps along the road to closing a sale.

- **Feeling good.** There is a strong relationship between how good we feel, and how well we sell. So, always be good to yourself and stay fit, dress reasonably well, and do not let work be the only focus of your life – otherwise you will not enjoy the benefits of hard work.

- **Finally,** whoever makes the decision to buy, and it is not always the obvious person, always try to involve them, ask and answer their questions, and make them feel good about you. It is generally the quiet ones you need to involve, but be subtle!

Success in selling will not depend upon specific techniques, but by finding your route to success and sticking to it. Yes, read books, and try new things, but experience takes time and patience, it depends upon where you place the emphasis, how you relate to people and yourself, your drive and motivation, and many variables. Once you have found your formula, stick to it. Do not think that you will have overnight success. Of course you may, and if you do then – this is fantastic, but if not then do not be disheartened. What was that old phrase?

If at first you don't succeed, try, try again.

If you need sales, understand the natural sales cycle and put the emphasis where it counts – right at the very beginning. And do not forget who the most important person is in all of this – it is, of course, the client.

8

Advertising

"Remember the 3 R's: Respect for self; Respect for others; and Responsibility for what you do!"

Everyone knows that to make people aware of your product or service you must advertise it. But this is easier said than done:

- Who do you try to influence?
- Where do you advertise?
- When do you advertise?
- What do you advertise, what do you say, and what are you trying to achieve?
- How do you do it, and how much do you spend?
- Why are you advertising in the first place?

Advertising does not automatically bring you more sales. It gets you noticed and helps ensure the people you meet are both informed and interested. Some advertising is effective; some is a waste of time. Your responsibility is to make your advertising as effective as possible, waste as little as possible.

Marketing, we have realised, is about knowing what people want, who your potential clients are, and therefore what your message to the market should be! Advertising is one way (albeit an important way) in which you put that message to the public. It gets you to meet more people, gets more into the sales machine, and selling is the converting of this activity into sales. It helps you feed the sales machine.

Many small companies are good at selling face to face, but somehow lack the skills and understanding to use advertising effectively. The problem they have is that they do not come into contact with enough people to sell to. In short, they have insufficient leads to drive the sales machine. Their business therefore cannot reach its potential.

However, by following some very simple rules and grasping some basic ideas, you can greatly improve the effectiveness of your promotional activities! How can you do this? Effective advertising, of course.

START AT THE BEGINNING

Let me start with a personal story. Everybody (well almost everybody) has heard of Pearl & Dean in England, the cinema advertisers who would trawl an area selling advertising for the cinema. What a magnet! To have your name up on the big screen alongside the latest blockbuster, and of course you could guarantee being in front of thousands of movie-goers. We were wooed by Pearl & Dean, bought an expensive ad, and it was shown alongside some excellent films! We too went to the movies, saw the excellent ad, and like all other advertisers, we expected more people through the door the next day. Many of our regulars complimented the advertisement, but few new customers (if any, to be honest) came to try us because of our marvellous advertisement. The ad failed; we were stunned. After all that effort and expense! Why, we asked, did the programme not work? Why, because our egos got the better of us.

We had failed to ask ourselves why we had chosen to advertise with Pearl & Dean, and had ignored four key questions:

- **What was being promoted?** We had failed to link the features and benefits of what we offered to the people who would be in the cinema, if they could be linked at all,

- **What do the viewers of the advertisements want?** Who were the viewers and ... what do they want, and why?

128

- **What were we trying to achieve?** Were we trying to sell ourselves to them, and the benefits of what we did, were we just trying to inform them we were there, or were we massaging our egos?

- **Had we considered the best way to achieve all of these?** Obviously in our case, this point had been completely missed!

We had wanted more clients to come through the door, but had failed to see that perhaps this was not the best media to achieve that. Perhaps the majority of cinema goers were totally apathetic to what went on in the breaks, were otherwise occupied ... and this is where we had best leave this particular story.

YOUR OBJECTIVES FROM ADVERTISING

As an advertiser, particularly if you have a small business, your objective of advertising is quite simple. You want to increase short term sales. Why else would you bother? Within this simple statement, there are four main reasons to advertise:

- To inform people who do not use you that they should. You must know who they are and how to contact them. This is very important for trying to break into the French market.

- To remind people who are (or may be) currently buying that, yes, they could be using you.

- To regain past clients lost to you, or more important, lost to others. For this you need to understand why they may have stopped buying.

- To let the world know you are still there, still in business, to ensure that you are not forgotten about!

THE LAW OF FOCUSED ATTENTION

A fundamental rule of advertising is to understand the kind of people who pay most attention to your advert. The Law of Focused Attention tells you just that!

This law says that, the people who pay most attention to your advertisement are the people who wrote it and paid for it – i.e. you and your colleagues or associates! You will read your advertisement avidly, and expect great things. Because you wrote it, you know what it says, and what it is supposed to mean. And because this is what you wanted to say, by God, it must be a good advertisement. It says just what you wanted, what a surprise. But is it a good advert? That is quite another question altogether.

Who else really reads advertisements? There are three basic types of readers, and two others who may come back and look for you afterwards:

- **Skimmers.** These are people who are attracted by headlines and things that catch the eye, people flicking through magazines, their eyes will pass over the ad, but without something to catch their attention; they will not see nor remember it.

- **Scanners.** These are people who scan various media (usually magazines) for interesting things that catch the eye, and who will read things that initially interest them.

- **Readers.** These are people who read everything and will take forever, but often just forget much of the detail in the plethora of information – try it yourself one day, read the magazine from cover to cover, as well as the advertisements, one by one, and see how many you can remember!

Of the others, these include:

- Bored people, who will flick through magazines (e.g. in the doctor's) because they have nothing better to do.

- People who are looking for specific items and are scanning back issues of magazines to find a useful contact who can help solve a problem.

So what can we learn from this? I believe that most small businesses write their adverts for readers when, in fact, most of their audience do not read what they write. The result is that most advertising is too detailed, too long, and doomed to failure. Completely ineffective! Indeed, many people will not see what you write simply because of the number of words they are confronted with. Nothing stands out; it looks hard to read, so it is ignored. What a waste!

Every advertisement must tell the whole story. Imagine nobody knows you, nobody understands you, they all have differing points of view to you. So to succeed you need the people who open the media to see your advertisement, and take notice. How do you achieve that?

- Your advert must stand alone and tell the story you want it to tell.

- You must know what this story is to start with!

- The words you use must be short, simple and 'human', and the people who see it must associate with the words you use.

- Humour is wasted; people do not buy from clowns. If you are trying to sell to people, understand that humour is generally appreciated only when you have got to know them as clients – and then only sparingly.

- Be restrained in your superlatives – I understand that you think you are the best at what you do, so there is really no need to tell me again, unless you are not really confident. Being too free with the use of superlatives only gives the impression of a lack of confidence, so be careful not only what you say, but also how your use of words is interpreted.

- Use the space well.

THOUGHTFUL USE OF SPACE

Using the space well is important. Although this may seem silly to say because it is intuitively obvious, few people put it into practice. When you buy advertising, you buy space, nothing else, and it is up to you what you do with it.

The normal reaction is to see how much you can cram into that space. Well, perhaps I exaggerate, but unfortunately this is how many people act, it seems. Especially here in France where there is less business support, and fewer people who can write the adverts for you. You are forced to rely on your own instincts, and this is where many people fall down.

Start by remembering that few people read what you write, unless they are interested, so if you write a lot then you are actively detracting from what you want to achieve. The space you have purchased for your advertising message has to do one thing above all others: it needs to grab people's attention, and get them interested. If it does not do that, then your advert has failed – people will not read your words. How do you grab people's attention? Well, simple – you write something that they will see *when it is set on a crowded page*, that will motivate them to contact you. This first rule is the hardest.

The second rule is perhaps counter-intuitive, and this is that there should be sufficient space around the words you write, adequate colour, and use of image to make what you write stand out. And of these, the most important is space. There is no special formula that I know of, but take a critical look at any magazine or newspaper, and pick out the advertisements that take you eye. What do you notice about them? Space!

Of course it is more than just space, but space is the starting point from which you will move to refine what you do. You might want blocks of colour, but for that you need space. Whatever you do to refine your advertisement and make it more attention grabbing, the more you will see the need for space.

This then brings in the subjects of benefits and costs. Working on the principle that advertising space costs money, the more space you buy, the more it costs. So, if you want space, and it is expensive (and costs must be controlled) refine what you say to bring it back to the absolute minimum. What do you feel will attract the attention of readers or viewers, even listeners if yours is a radio advert, and make it clear. Trying to decrease the amount of space needed for words by refining your message has the implicit benefit that you need to really think about *what* you are saying. This means that anything, yes absolutely anything, that detracts from, or conceals, your main message should be eliminated. If in doubt, cut it out!

Finally, your advertisement should tell the reader or listener what to do next, whether to phone you now, keep your number for emergencies, visit your showroom, or whatever you are trying to convince them to do. The outcome of every good advertisement is a call for people to do something, a call to action. Apathy rules. People are lazy. If you do not tell them to do something, the chances are that they will do nothing!

Unfortunately for advertisers, the majority of people have limited attention spans. If you ask people to do something now, they may well do it. If they wait until later, they will probably forget. If you make people do something, this reinforces your message, and the effect of your advertisement will be so much more powerful, it will be remembered. This 'call to action' is what makes a good advertisement, and explains why your advert needs to be so much more effective than others.

THE LAZY Z

However you lay out your advertisements, it helps to know how people look at what is presented to them. Try looking at any printed matter, and when you scan the page trace the way your eyes move. Typically you will find that because English is written top left of the page to bottom right, and habits are (after all) habits, the path of the eye follows a Z down the page. Yes, on a large page there may be several Zs, one atop the other, but this path will be followed in the vast majority of cases. The same is true of individual adverts, the advert that catches the eye will be skimmed, and the eye will follow this Z pattern.

This has several key implications when laying out advertisements. These are simple, and provide guides for an effective layout of an advert:

- The first line must grab the reader's attention, else all is potentially lost.

- Key points in addition are highlighted, and on the Z.

- The action point is clear, usually at the bottom of the space.

Armed with this tip, cast your eyes quickly over several pages of advertising, and look both at the ones that attract you, and at the ones that seem 'not to work' for you or are unclear. Learning to write good advertising 'copy' is sometimes best done by criticising the work of others (good and bad), then when you have had a go, get someone to criticise yours.

What does this mean for you? Well, armed with the knowledge that this is what happens, knowing that to allow space you must ensure effective writing, and the knowledge of what you want readers to do, you can begin to play with advertising layouts that suit what you do and what you want. Remember the need for clarity and simplicity, keep things clear and uncluttered. The judge of a good advertisement is the reader, not you, and they vote with their feet!

FEATURES AND BENEFITS

Somewhere in everybody's decision to purchase, they decide around features and benefits, and balance this with the cost. Only in fashion and status items do people buy just features, because that brings the benefit of either being fashionable or being 'one up'. So do not forget the benefits.

People buy benefits. 'Same day delivery' is not in itself a benefit. From your client's point of view, same day delivery is a feature that for them means no lost time, fewer delays, lower costs, more satisfied customers, good service, indeed a whole stack of things that are almost irrelevant to you in some respects. In this case the feature of what you offer is same day delivery, but the benefits that brings will depend on your client.

People usually buy the benefits that things bring to them; it answers the "What's in it for me?" question, "Why bother with this ad?" This then surely has a consequence for you as someone writing your own adverts! The headline (the thing that grabs attention) should:

- Be complete in itself, and be understandable.
- Be easy to understand.
- Use common language.
- Convey the ideas of benefits – to your reader.

WAYS TO IMPROVE WRITING FOR ADVERTS

There are always opportunities to improve, and what is good one day will be different the next. However there are ten clear ground rules that you need to follow, if you want to improve how your advertisements are written. These are:

1. Do not consider yourself clever, nor above your audience – it *will* show in what you write, and people hate 'clever buggers'.

2. Do not take for granted that your audience knows your technology, few are interested, and all they want are the benefits!

3. Use words that are pleasing – academics make lousy advertisers, so do most politicians! It isn't always easy!

4. Be specific – use the scalpel savagely while cutting down on what you write.

5. Be controversial, people never remember you if you do not stand out.

6. Use repetition, and keep an advert running for a while before you judge success.

7. Start with a benefit.

8. Put benefits in the middle.

9. And of course, end with benefits, and finally.

10. Use short words and forget being technical.

ADVERTISING MEDIA

Here in France, as everywhere, there are various forms of advertising media that relate to the markets or groups of people that you are trying to communicate with. For the English entrepreneur, you are more limited in some ways, yet have more options in other ways. Certainly, because you have fewer options, you can guarantee that your audience too has fewer options.

Whatever you do, there are some forms of advertising that are very important and traditionally are used by all groups, English and French. The most important of these is the sign writing on your vehicles, which traditionally is a good advert for you when they are parked. For artisans it also overcomes the problem that you should have a sign outside every 'chantier' or workplace, both for deliveries and so that the authorities can check on you if needed. The French typically are much better at using interesting artwork for sign writing, and vehicles are generally much prettier than in England, but they often forget the need to remember ...

Who you are, what you do, and how to contact you.

The internet is great for advertising, but how often do we see a complex name at aol.com, or gmail.com, or even yahoo.fr (or was that yahoo.com)? Having a website, or an email address, does not guarantee that people will be able to remember it, and hence be able to visit your site or contact you. Nor are typical web addresses even written in a way that makes it easy for people to remember them. A long string of letters written in lower case is hard to decipher. Some years ago I purchased the address, www.oldkingcole.co.uk, which is not intuitive and easy to remember when first seen. So I decided always to write this using capitals www.OldKingCole.co.uk, which becomes much easier to recall, especially as my name is ... Cole.

Websites can be a good advertisement, and they should be both interesting and informative. Yet too many are simple (often disinteresting) pages put on somebody else's server, and are very difficult to find. I have several classic examples on my desk. I tried to find one of them on the web from memory, and after several attempts I gave up on a complex business name, with a site at fusiveweb.co.uk, sorry. I also found another at chez-alice.fr difficult when there was not even a www in front of the address. Look, I may be stupid in many ways, but in my view, if the internet is supposed to be easy, why make it difficult. Sorry, but it makes me so mad when people make such elementary mistakes, because if this is the reaction of typical customers, you will be wasting your time.

Not every person can have a web address that is memorable, but it is so much more professional when you do, or you make efforts to ensure memorability. There are plenty of places where you can purchase them, and for little cost you can have an email address or website address that people can remember, and therefore can find.

There are many English language websites that offer advice, forums and the opportunity to advertise, the best known across France seems to be www.AngloInfo.com. The site seems to be very popular where we are, but you should ask locally what sites are available and popular where you live. If a site is well known, it shows that your advert will stand a better chance of being seen. There are many specialist sites as well, especially for holiday accommodation; you will have to judge the benefits these could bring. I personally find some of these sites difficult as, without being biased, it is not clear what they offer. You must judge the quality of websites for yourself.

I was always taught the value of using shoe leather. When we started a company in England, we were advised that it would be a good idea to canvas local companies, just knock on doors and explain what we planned to do. It paid dividends, not only did people know what we would be doing; they appreciated the obvious efforts we made. Our business grew topsy turvy, doubling in size every few months. It worked for us, and it can work for you too, despite the issue of language. OK, your business may require you to think around the problems of how to make this work for you, but surely you are able to do that. Personal introduction is always valuable, you are not then 'faceless'.

You may consider leaflets put on local cars, possibly in town centres, possibly at local supermarkets, even leafleting at local markets could be very useful. Leaflets are definitely cost effective if they work, and many computer programmes allow you to design you own leaflets when you start. You can physically hand your leaflets out, face to face, according to where you feel your business will be strong. You can even tour an area, although this takes time, or ask 'la Poste' to include your leaflet the next time they deliver publicity (again there is a cost).

All ports and airports have leaflet stands, you could try leaving leaflets here. Certain periods of the year are more popular with tourists, but low cost air travel ensures a steady stream through airports. Leaflets, as an advertising media, must follow the golden rules for layout and content!

Our first big job in France came because somebody saw our leaflet on someone else's car ... and took it! Many thousand Euros worth of work came at an opportune time, just from the use of feet! Would we repeat the effort now? Well that depends the amount of work we have!

Consider the use of posters, perhaps in local shops or in Mairies (the centre of every commune), they can prove very beneficial. Boulangeries are especially important in France, they are a place where many people go for bread, a key ingredient for every meal. To get established when we arrived in France, (the story is too long to tell here), we got involved helping with French language groups for the English living locally. Placing posters in a variety of situations, often boulangeries (bread shops, sorry) proved highly effective. Being in English, naturally, we explained what the poster was for to the French ladies who worked there. I know that they pointed them out to English customers, especially those that spoke little or no French. Not only did we get the poster well situated, but also personal encouragement from the staff! We also got to taste some great bread, although it did little for the waistline.

PR (as it is known) has always been a good way to get known locally, but effectiveness varies. There are few newspapers and magazines targeted at the English, and writing articles as PR has started to lose appeal to the English language media providers it would seem, although an advert placed with the article could pave the way and open doors. They are always interested in their revenue! Telephone the relevant magazine and ask the question. When you are writing PR articles, it pays to use those words that grab attention. If you have never written professionally, either employ the services of a PR consultant, or find somebody (such as a journalist) who understands what sells papers.

Telling French newspapers that you have something interesting to offer them is often a good way to get visibility in the French market. Local French newspapers have much less (if any) advertising I have found, and are well read locally (possibly because of this). Many locals read papers for local news and events, and you will see crowds of people reading them in supermarkets. You will not be the judge of what is included, and you must have something to say, or have done something that is newsworthy. Having said that, if you can get stories into the French newspapers, that will give you good exposure, although you will need to follow this up with advertisements, and expect contact from potential customers in French! Not the easiest over the phone.

Until fairly recently, there was a national English language newspaper, *French News*, and although this no longer exists, there are rumours of others thinking of filling the gap.

Local coverage is patchy for magazines, so you will need to look carefully at what is available in your area. Speak to English residents and ask how they source services, what they read, and where they purchase newspapers.

Oddly the notice boards in the large/local supermarkets are read by many people. However, the fear of reading French puts many English residents off notice boards, and because of the size of the country, reaching English residents could prove a challenge.

English people with holiday homes, or simple tourists, can be more difficult groups to reach. Obviously you can contact hotels and property owners, but this is time consuming. The target market are usually based in England, so perhaps one route to consider is the specialist press for people with homes (or wanting homes) in France. This route is usually expensive, but cost is always relative. French Property News always seemed to be well read. There is (of course) the media promoted by the likes of Brittany Ferries, but again advertising here is not cheap, and can be hit and miss. Some magazines such as Brit Mag leave free copies in ports on the north coast of France, as well as airports in Brittany.

French speakers have a much more diverse selection of media, much the same as in the UK, including free advertising papers, local papers, magazines, radio, brochures, posters, indeed all the options open in the UK, but with a French flavour adapted to your locality. You could try these, if you are trying to attract French clients.

What about other options and ideas? Well coming to France you will need to be creative to achieve what you want, Try some of these ideas, there will be many more.

- Referrals – what's wrong with asking satisfied clients or even local people who they think you should go to see, even possible clients who would benefit from your work? Get proactive and contact them before they have thoughts of doing the work themselves or using others! It can be slower than other ways of becoming known, but is effective.

- How about writing an 'agony aunt' column in an English speaking magazine – it usually brings no income but probably is good publicity. Or start a publicity vehicle yourself!

- You could run 'surgeries' at the village hall (the Salle Polyvalente). An excellent source of work if this is appropriate. Or you could take a stall at a local event!

- Concentrate on a few niche skills where you can grow a reputation. Word will spread quickly, helped along of course by you.

- Do something outrageous – one builder locally advertised himself as 'Jean Pierre et fille' (the 'et fille' being 'and daughter'). From this he got loads of attention if only from the ladies, who are (after all) about 50% of the population, and are seriously important in the decision process! Whether he turned this into work I do not know, but he had the opportunity. What is to stop you doing something unusual!

The more you think about it, the more ways there are to communicate. Seriously, if there are no routes to advertise, you may even consider starting some advertising media yourself – everyone else in the area will have the same problems as you, businesses and people looking for traders and services, or route to the market. For sure, watching the television and hoping the phone will ring is perhaps not the best way to gain sales. Shoe leather, telephoning, whatever, there will always be ways to put your message across. That's advertising. Who said it would be easy?

KEEPING UP THE PRESSURE

Most small businesses in France, both English and French, have the endless problem of finding work when they are busy. That takes discipline. It is not easy be selling when you're doing, and you can't be doing when you're out selling.

Doing the work is that it brings in the money, and is often more fun than selling after all. So it's easy to see why sales get forgotten. Feeding the sales machine takes time, and you must allow time for selling now to overcome future famine later. If it means time must be better managed – then manage your time. If you do not feed the machine, you will have all the time in the world.

9

Pricing – How much should I charge?

"How long is a piece of string?
As long as you want to make it!"

Many businesses say that it's tough out there, and customers want the lowest price. It does not take a genius to understand that people do not want to pay more than necessary, why then do prices vary, and often the most successful – and sought after – companies have charges above the minimum. For businesses that have really not thought through what they do, and what they offer, only too often price cuts are an easy way out; effectively you are 'buying' work.

Pricing is a balance, and you should be both fair to yourself and the client. If you are fair, you will win in the longer term. What you can get as reward for your efforts must be matched by your ability and willingness to do a good job, and the better you are at meeting your client needs, the more comfortable your clients will be at paying you what you all think and agree is a fair price.

Fairness in business is important. It does not mean low cost, or even that you cannot make good profits; but everybody must feel they are being treated fairly. That way you will get more work, and you work well for the client. Everybody wins.

Issues that you need to consider and include when pricing work in France will include:

- The size of the country and distances you must travel to work travel, which with rising energy prices increases the cost to you. Experience shows that English artisans and traders need to be more willing to travel to get work, as the English in France tend to be geographically spread.

- Inconvenience and when the client needs the work done, including emergency callouts, night and weekend work and working to clients' schedules (for example, their holiday schedules!).

There are English businesses out here that charge their English customers more because they know the customers are afraid (or unable) to speak French and will therefore turn to the first available English suppliers or artisans – leaving themselves open to people who are less ethical. It happens.

Things that generally increase prices include:

- **Urgency.** Your help is it needed *now* – for example, a 'fosse septique' (septic tank) needs emptying today as the toilets are blocked – not unheard of in France. It often narrows purchasers' choice to companies carrying greater costs who are more expensive.

- **Luxury** items always carry a premium price, for example pools and saunas, as there are fewer suppliers in a limited market,

- **Choice** – if you are the only supplier for a particular service, you can of course charge a premium, but high prices encourage others to start in the same business and undercut you, creating a longer term problem,

- **Danger or discomfort.** Dirty and dangerous jobs invariably have a premium.

- If something becomes '**fashionable**', and options are limited, the prices go up. Alternative energy including solar panels are a possible example here, as popularity and interest exists, but as yet there are few suppliers, when people expect to either pay a premium and possibly grants are available to offset higher cost.

- **Fashion items** in the traditional sense, with media exposure, makes more people from a certain group want what is on offer. Greater demand often reduces availability and pushes up price, and if there is a limited life cycle of what you have on offer, you will need to make your profits while you have the chance!

- **Need** is a good driver, and a classic example of this is ice cream on a hot day at the seaside. A quality ice cream, a brand leader, can cost over six times the supermarket cost in a special kiosk. You are hot and need to cool down. So you pay the price asked. Worse, you have children and they are clamouring for an ice cream, you pay the price for peace and quiet. On cooler days you are naturally shocked at the mark-up that these charlatans are hoping to make. But when you need an ice cream, where else can you go?

- **Quality** always has a price tag attached to it. Hotels are good examples of this. A beach-side 5-star luxury hotel naturally charges substantially more than the local B&B. It is expected, the price is paid, and anyway, those who can afford the luxury want to set themselves apart from those that cannot. Yet there is nothing to stop a good B&B charging a premium for services above standard, and moving towards 'the top end of the market'.

- **Surroundings and location** can and do influence price dramatically. Things that increase perceived value include ease of access, proximity to towns or beaches, located in cities or tourist areas etc. It is odd, but mostly it is the business person who identifies these key issues. What can you identify about your location?

Remember, there are things that will decrease perception of quality or value, even though this may not actually be the case. They are often variations of the things in the list above, but while fashion drives up price, popularity can also drive it down. Also, if people wish to use your service with regularity, there is an expectation that the price will come down.

An example of this is the Basque restaurant local to us, an auberge that sells excellent food and the normal menu is quite expensive. The lunchtime trade, though, attracts regular diners – something obviously to be encouraged. Yet lunchtime diners will not pay restaurant prices, so there is a 'plat du jour' (dish of the day), picked from their menu, which is put out at a fraction of the price. This is seen as good value, and attracts the diners. The restaurant is full, not empty. Profit margins are lower, but at least a profit is being made.

Profit all boils down to a few simple things, all of which are interconnected. These revolve around three core issues:

1. How much you do.
2. How much you charge for doing it.
3. What your costs are.

There is little point in trying to do more work if, at the end of the day, all you get is more work and less reward. Without profit there is no point in being in business. When pricing your goods please remember that you are in business to make money, even if you are a charity. Yes, charities also need to make a profit so that they can use this to benefit others. Price accordingly. If you make a profit and your business grows, so that you make more profit – as we all know, that is what business is about. If you cut price to grow, or do not charge enough in the first place, then you are on a hiding to nothing. What you do with your profits is up to you.

THE INFLUENCE OF PRICE

Price does influence the way your product is seen in relation to competition, the volume of sales you may have, the amount of service you can afford to give to customers, the profit you make, your quality of life, the motivation of any staff you employ, your own self esteem, and much more. What you charge touches everything and is central to your business and your life. It speaks volumes about your business, which is turn speaks volumes about you.

If you offer low prices, people assume you work to lower standards, lower quality, and therefore your product is not as good. That's life. Low cost will not stop customers complaining, if what you do is poor. Profit can only be dirty word if you let it be, and although few people want to actively help you make it, everyone realizes that when you are in business then, you must make a profit to stay in business. You must price accordingly.

Ethics have nothing to do with earning a profit; they do have an impact on what you do with it!

Let us look at two garages, both in France, but it does not really matter where they are as this holds true anywhere.

- One will do all sorts of work for you at no extra charge. The owner is a nice guy, a very knowledgeable mechanic, always smiles and talks politely, but his business is the same as it has been for years. His hourly rate is low, and there is never any investment; he always seemingly struggles to make ends meet, his staff are dressed in oily overalls. You go to him for the basic work or when you do not know what the problem is exactly, because you know he will do good job, not charge too much, and probably check a few extra odds and sods. You can always get the car booked in within days and he will never run up a big bill; he knows you'd complain if he did.

- Then there is the other garage, a main dealer. The staff is of variable quality (from very good to dubious) and some are only able to change parts, rather than repair things. Hourly rates are high, and jobs are costed on how long the manufacturer says the work should take – and you often wonder how jobs can be made to take that long. They are always busy. You go to this garage when you want an important job done. Always there is a big bill, but you expect that and so don't complain.

There's a message in this, and it isn't too hard to see when you look at price as an issue.

DO NOT UNDERVALUE YOURSELF

Profit is what is left after you have paid yourself. So you have to cover your costs, buy your materials, pay yourself and still make a profit. It is only too easy to forget this profit element, or confuse yourself into thinking that the profit element is what you pay yourself. Profit is what is left after you have paid yourself.

Many people undervalue their efforts, and sell themselves short. You need to reinforce the idea of value, both in your own and your customer's minds. To do so takes the mind off cost. You must then build the value you add into the price you charge.

Let me recount a story.

Some years ago a businessman was forced from his country and came to England with nothing. A few pounds and the clothes he had on, together with his family. He had to make a living. So he leased a shop, and opened for business. There was not much in the shop, but it was clean. You could have eaten from the floors it was so clean. When asked for something he didn't have, he apologized and said "Sorry, but if you are going to be a regular customer, I will stock it for you." Market research as he was going along! His shops got busier and busier.

He had noticed one key point. In England there is no such thing as a fixed price. So our friend recognized that he could charge a premium on some items and make a good profit. He stayed open late, and people were sure he would stock the things they wanted so they shopped there. When they wanted earlier opening, he did that too. Everything was tailored to his customers' needs. But he was not cheap. Why should he be? He was providing a service the customers valued.

Now he has a chain of smaller local supermarkets around the West Midlands. He has 'made it'.

You can do it too. It is not difficult to make a profit if you are in business, the rule is ...

Find out what your customers want and provide it at a profit.

The man starting with the small supermarkets recognized the need for cleanliness and service with flexible and long opening hours. Identify what it is your customers want. Give customers what they want and charge for it.

WHAT COULD YOU CHARGE

What you should really charge is simple to say, but hard to work out. Charge what the market will stand. You can see market pricing all around you, and on some things pricing is easy, but others it can be very difficult to know what you can 'get away with'.

Let us take the classic example of eating out in France, and compare the fashionable café and the 'ouvriers (workers) restaurant' or 'relais', a more basic everyday place to eat at lunchtime offering a 4 or 5-course meal for around €10, about £8.

Why are some places able to charge more money for smaller portions, and the relais provides a good 5-course meal for less money than the price of one item elsewhere! Yes, in the latter the menu is limited, perhaps basic, but the volumes and quality is good. They are popular, crowded, but while turnover is higher, workloads are greater, and profit per meal is much lower.

The relais must be very busy, and price limits the profit. High turnover, low cost is the business model they follow. If regular customers want good inexpensive food, then if you charge too much you are bound to fail. If you can find a location where people want different food such as tourist areas, cities or you offer a specialist menu, then why not go up-market.

The world of fashion is similar. A piece of cloth in some shops sells for a premium when it has a designer label on it. A very similar piece of cloth without the label obviously coming in from the Far East sells for much lower cost. Where is the difference in value? Well it must be in the mind of the beholder, because in modern economies, and in an effort to maximise profits, many well known labels will make their garments in a similar factory in the Far East. Indeed, the only difference is perhaps the label and one minor detail!

Price can have little to do with quality of manufacture. Of course you do not expect an expensive piece to be poorly made, but many inexpensive pieces are equally well made.

Do not be ashamed of thinking that your product (or service) is of higher value than your competitors. If you don't, then your clients never will!

THE VOLUME/PRICE TRADE-OFF

There is always going to be a trade-off between volume and price. As your price increases, so fewer people will either want or be able to pay for your services. Also, if people give you a lot of work, they may ask for (and expect) some kind of discount. This is normal. There is no right answer. What you decide to do is up to you, and the outcome often depends upon the amount of work you have.

But there are things to consider. Do not feel that you have to reach, nor sell to everyone – you must target your market. You should not want to do business with everybody. You probably couldn't anyway. That way you become a busy fool. Remember the sums. Your costs can even go up as volume of turnover increases. If your price comes down even a little, then volume may have to increase substantially to even maintain current profit levels.

As an example, let's say John sells boxes at £10 each. With a Net Profit of 10% he makes £1 clear profit on each box. Imagine he cuts his price by 5%, perhaps because he has an idea that his boxes are too expensive, or someone else has told him he's too dear, or because a competitor has cut his price, or even he has had a brainstorm. His costs stay the same at first, so now he only makes 50p per box. He will have to double sales to keep profit levels up to past levels. Then come the hidden consequences. Because he needs to make twice as many boxes he needs more cash for materials and must borrow from the bank. Interest and other charges put more pressure on profit. He has to employ more box makers and salesmen who are not yet experienced. Sales staff need cars, which require up-front costs – more money from the bank. And so it goes on, John has seen profit eliminated simply by reducing his price by a small amount. Oh, and what has happened to turnover? Has he sold more boxes? Well, local competitors have all reduced their price to stay competitive, but because there is a limited demand for boxes, the number of boxes sold stays the same. John's stocks have gone up, costs have gone up, staff have gone up, temperature's gone up, and the only thing to go down has been profit.

It is well to be busy. Stay busy, but not to be a busy fool, and not at any cost. Remember as well this old adage,

Turnover is vanity, profit is sanity.

THE PRICING MATRIX

There is one simple tool that may help in setting your prices: the Pricing Matrix. This is simply a grid comparing what you and competitors charge. Let me give you an example of how it works. It is effective because it is very easy, and flexible. You simply list out your competitors down one side of a piece of paper, put your products and services across the top, and then fill in the grid with the prices, as in the example that follows.

Imagine your five competitors, companies A, B, C, D and E. None do *exactly* the same as you, but all operate in the same field. There are four basic product types (numbered 1 – 4) for convenience. It should not be beyond the wit of man to find out how much each charge for a product group. There are always guides within industries, and if you cannot find exact comparisons, you can make value judgements. This is simple for products but can be just as effective when dealing with even quite complex services or even charges for time. It makes no difference how many products or how many competitors you have; just the bigger it gets and the longer it takes.

Price Matrix

Competitor	Product 1	Product 2	Product 3	Product 4
Comp A	€2.50		€3.75	
Comp B	€4.00	€6.00	€3.50	
Comp C		€7.10	€2.90	€6.75
Comp D	€5.50			€5.50
Comp E		€5.00	€1.90	

From the grid above we can compare prices for comparable products and services from all our local competitors. How can you apply this kind of idea? I always recommend the 'upper quartile' approach. Using this approach, we can work out where we want to pitch our products.

UPPER QUARTILE

What, you may ask, is a quartile? Well, in simple terms, it is a quarter of any scale, a quarter of any range. This scale could easily be the scale of what people charge, from the cheapest to the most expensive which is the situation that applies here. So, the upper quartile is that area between 3/4 and the top of the charging rates. It is the 'upper quarter of the scale'. Perhaps the area that you should be looking to aim for with your prices is not the top, because that does make you look expensive. Somebody has to be best and somebody the most expensive, although these are not always the same. You could aim to be not too far from the top. The person at the top of the scale, probably a market leader will be known and respected, but if you are a little less expensive, you could do well! And remember, higher prices give the impression of quality – and nobody wants poor quality work. Never forget the subtle impressions that prices have – higher is good quality, lower prices give the impression of poorer quality.

From the grid above, what sort of prices could you ask? Well, for me, I would charge just short of the top, but do as good a job as the person at the top ... or better perhaps. I would certainly try to offer a better or more personable service. Perhaps for Product 1, around £5, Product 2 around £6.50, Product 3 around £3.50 and Product 4 around the £6.50 mark. Without giving it too much thought, provided your quality is good, your pricing becomes easier. You can of course make adjustments, but as a guide this works well. Of course, you could choose to price lower, but why would you want to do that?

You alone will know whether you are able to put your business out at that price at a profit. However, if this is the market you have chosen, and if your prices are close to the top, you should make a profit. If not there is something wrong! If this is the case, you have chosen the wrong business, or should not be in business!

"Ah," I hear you say, "how can I justify these prices?" Easy, the additional services you offer justify the price. And to understand just what that is means you need to know what your customer wants. The nice thing about setting your prices higher is that you can always bring your prices down, but it is difficult to raise then if you start too low!

This is only a guide, albeit an effective one. But remember that price is determined by supply and demand, and you may need to lower prices if there are too many people chasing too little work – or look elsewhere to start your business. The reverse is also true, too little supply and prices can go up, as the following story demonstrates.

THE PARABLE OF THE FORD ESCORT

There are several pricing stories, but this one has stayed in my mind. It sums up the practical ideas of price and supply in everyday language, words that everybody relates to. It is called the 'Parable of the Ford Escort', and relates to the experience of (I believe) a man in Derby.

One day a man decided to fix the left back light of his wife's Ford Escort, probably for its MOT test. It could be a Citroen or whatever in France, the principle is the same. The price asked by the local Ford dealership seemed ridiculous for just a piece of plastic held on by several screws; it was well over £100, I recall. We've all had to buy that simple part which we feel is a rip off, and yes, you naturally look for other options. So taking his life in both hands, almost like stepping into alien territory, this man decided to go to a local scrap merchant. Actually, there were about five car-breakers close together, so he was confident that he would get what he wanted there.

At the first of these breakers, he went in and asked how much the light was. "Oh, they're £20, but we haven't got one to fit that model, try Charlie's down the road." Thanking him for his help, he went to Charlie's where he got much the same response. "Oh, they're £20, but we haven't got one to fit that model, try next door." The story was the same at the other three yards as well. £20 each, but nobody had one.

Disappointed, he was resigned to buying a new fitting when he remembered Yellow Pages. There he found a car-breaker, quite local, who specialized in Fords. He rang them up and, yes, they had the part. "Put one by for me, I'm on my way."

On arriving he went straight to the counter and asked for the piece he needed, which was handed to him, all clean and tidy. "That'll be £30, please," said the man behind the counter. "£30, that's a bit dear" said our friend. "Every other scrap man said the price was only £20." So the man behind the counter asked where he had been, whom he had seen and what had been said.

"Did they have one to sell to you?" the man behind the counter finally asked. "No," our friend admitted. "Then I'll tell you. When I haven't got one the price will be £20, and I'd be willing to save one for you, but today I have, and the price to you is £30. Or, if you want, you can go to the dealer and buy a new one."

That is the Parable of the Ford Escort. Hidden in there are some very important messages that you would do well to ponder. There are many elements of good business sense in being street wise!

WHAT IF PRICE IS KEY

If price is absolutely vital, for example in a tendering environment (where you are giving a competitive price for certain services), then you do have to be sharper on your pricing. And the only way you can be that, is to look very carefully at what is needed, provide just what is asked... and cut your costs accordingly. In France, you are often held to your quote, called 'le devis' in French – and this should not vary unless there are changes beyond your control.

Be creative and look for opportunity, be careful how you parcel things together, and be very specific on quality and materials. Obviously experience will tell you that there are likely to be problems, and it is here where you really stand to make some money – or help somebody out a problem so they owe you lots of favours and more profitable jobs elsewhere. If someone asks for a price for a specific job, and then changes the specification IN ANY WAY once work has started, you are free to charge more. For those that are very keen on low cost quotes that is always the problem they face.

A problem you could face working in France is one of language, and dealing with the French, your quote or 'devis' will possibly be in French. It can be difficult to argue changes in a foreign language, but if you are working for or with the English, especially once you have become established, you are on an equal footing. Equally important, if changes do occur, and you have a good relationship with a client, irrespective of language, problems should not occur.

KNOWN VALUE ITEMS

A similar kind of situation in competitive retailing is that of known value items. These things must be seen as competitive, simply because everyone knows the sort of price to expect. The 'typical shopping basket' is a good example of this in practice. Some products have a known price, and these prices are at the forefront of the decision maker's mind when deciding where to shop.

There are, however, other items that are sold where the supplier prices and profits rise significantly. When you go to your supermarket, ask yourself, of the items in your shopping trolley, which prices you know, even within 5%. Other than the basic products, the chances are that you will know few of the other prices, will just accept that the prices are right, and the supermarket competitive.

You could do as supermarkets do, and keep prices on certain items down, but make your profits on associated lines. You might sell (for example) low-cost fishing rods, then make your money on the paraphernalia associated such as bags, nets, bait, floats, indeed anything else that fishermen need. It is then down to you to be creative in the way you describe and sell these high price lines.

If you are dealing in areas where prices are well known, to increase you profit you should reduce your costs. Try considering these:

- Find alternative, cheaper suppliers of the same (or similar) products. This may involve using a slightly different or lower specification, or just shopping around. Prices for decorating materials are an example. Some wallpapers and paints are cheaper from volume retailers than to buy direct from the manufacturer. The same will also true of other things. Do not assume you are automatically getting the best deal from a manufacturer.

- Speak to your suppliers. Tell them their prices make you uncompetitive, that without some movement on price you will have to shop elsewhere. If you are having problems with their high prices then, if their charges are the same for everyone, all the other people who buy from them will be having problems too. The supplier's trade could be seriously affected.

- Look at other ways of cutting your costs, which could involve:
  - Different order volumes, buying more or buying with other retailers (as a group) to get volume discounts.
  - Perhaps having orders delivered, as a cheaper alternative to shopping yourself, possibly saving the cost of employing someone.

- Look for other services that can add to the package, or other products that you can sell, so that the costs you incur are spread, and effectively are reduced in proportion. If you only sell one product, all your fixed costs are focused on these and you are vulnerable. Selling other (compatible) things should spread your costs over a variety of products. It offers the chance, when one line doesn't sell, to sell other things instead, makes for a less risky business.

Pricing is an art. It is down to knowing your markets, what people want and what clients will pay. It is nothing more than that. Well, that and your confidence you can make your prices stick.

10

Staffing issues

"Don't let a little dispute injure a great friendship!"

This chapter is for background information and your guidance only, and is not meant to be definitive. In any staffing, contractual or legal issues, we strongly advise that you get, and take the advice of experts in the field of Human Resources and/or an advocate. As in the UK, the law and politics surrounding this whole area is complicated. The information here may help you to ask the professionals appropriate questions as befits your situation, and if we stop you running headlong into doing something that you will later regret, and take sound advice before proceeding, then we have succeeded.

France is a truly socialist state, no matter what the colour of the government. France has a history of extremely strong unions, protected groups such as the farmers, truckers and state employees, and a huge and bureaucratic civil service. Around half all employment being state sponsored or subsidized, it will not be easy to bring about change.

France (we are told) is trying to move away from the 35hr week; laws have been passed, but with difficulty and concessions to unions. Some employers and small business people, such as our local mayor who runs a busy enterprise, are less polite. He sees progress as two steps forward and three back, but it is early days. There is movement, and in the longer term we shall be better able to judge success.

What people want from a career in France is often different than in England, and there is definitely less raw ambition. Talking to a young lady we were aghast to learn her ambitions and career plans. She has a Masters Degree in Marketing, speaks English fluently, and could converse well in several other languages. Having spent years qualifying, her ambitions were to work for a Mairie (a town hall, run by the Mayor – the local administrative centre, with one in every commune), simply because the hours were good, she would have excellent time off with pregnancies of which she envisaged more than one, and retirement on a good pension at the age of 55. Hers is a typical story, which sadly speaks volumes about ambition, job security and employee rights – all of which are effectively subsidized by the state and ultimately the private sector employer.

Ah, you say, there are people like that everywhere, and yes, there are. It is, though, not an unusual story, as we had occasion to find this out when we visited St Ilan Agricultural College. Speaking to students in one particular year that had just returned from a summer project in England and Ireland, only one had what we would call ambition and wanted his own business. The others, though, were already considering the advantages of early retirement, a short working week and holidays. True, things may change, and change may be forced upon some of the students. But to consider the advantages of retirement as a teenager?

This is not trying to say that the French are bad employees; many work hard and are very proud to work for considerate employers, especially if in positions of authority. However, in a commercial world, employment rights can be very costly to small businesses. Certainly it helps keep unemployment high, putting many people off employing staff on an even remotely permanent basis.

One easy way around the responsibilities and costs is to use agency staff, and there are many employment agencies who will supply short term staff. This allows you the flexibility to increase workforce if you need in the short term, without serious consequences. Another option is to employ people as sub-contractors if this is appropriate.

LEGAL 'MUSTS' WHEN EMPLOYING

When you employ someone, they have rights as an employee, and you have rights (even in France) as an employer. Your rights are based upon what you both agree to do for each other, and so, to ensure that both parties fully understand their mutual obligations, there needs to be a contract of employment. With no formal contract, if there is a dispute, the courts always look sympathetically to the employee.

Now you can effectively employ someone with a verbal agreement, or just start them doing something that just continues through time, even just paying them cash (highly dubious but done). We are entering a grey area. The law will assume that you have a verbal agreement, and that they have a proper job, with normal industry rights – and that you have the proper responsibilities of an employer. Your position is almost secondary in some respects, as the rights of the employee are protected. As soon as you pay someone to do a job, unless they are self-employed, they become an employee.

Typically employment contracts need to cover all aspects of what you expect from the employee, and clearly must state mutual requirements. This is not important in the good times, when it may seem almost a waste of time and money; however it becomes vital when things start to go wrong. Any employee can become belligerent. Without a written contract, you have not specified what you expect from an employee and in the bad times they can (and will) just hold up their hands and shrug. People that have been the best of friends suddenly become antagonistic towards each other, and 'sorry' becomes a difficult word to say. Do not believe that it could not happen to you.

All French employment contracts must have the following information as a minimum, similar to requirements in the UK:

- A job description and job title that sets out clearly what you expect and what the employee's role and responsibilities are.

- The salary and perks that they will be due, and the hours they are expected to work (including holidays), including any flexibility needed and agreed for anti-social hours.

- Any general agreements that relate to the employment in this trade.

- Notice period in case of resignation.

- Places of work.

- The duration of the contract, if it is for a limited term.

TYPES OF EMPLPYMENT CONTRACT

In France there are two basic types of employment contract, those with a limited term known as a CDD (Contrat à Durée Déterminée) or a contract with no time limits, a normal job in other words, known as a CDI (Contrat à Durée Indéterminée).

Contrat à Durée Indéterminée (CDI)

This is a contract for a permanent job with no end-date, and it is what every employee really wants. There are many benefits that come with such a contract. Any new job usually has a two or three month trial period, which can be renewed if necessary, but this must be written into the contract, otherwise it does not officially exist. Both parties may choose to end the contract, and any notice period must be adhered to, although good reason must be given by the employer for termination. In reality, in France, it is very difficult for an employer to dispense with the services of an average employee unless the employee wants to go or does things illegal!

In order to encourage employers to take on younger staff into full time (rather than temporary) jobs, there are some incentives and grants. This is usually only for people aged up to 25, often disadvantaged, and conditions do apply, so ask at the local ANPE office for further information. You are generally looking at under-qualified people, or people living in a depressed area where jobs are harder to find. If you are looking to employ somebody, when you visit ANPE it would be wise to get the help of someone who can speak good English and French, just to ensure you understand your responsibilities!

If you do want to employ someone, a typical way in which employees are found is via the local network, perhaps the son of the friend of a friend, that way there is less likelihood of the employee being difficult (unless you are a poor boss). Many English employers tend to take on British workers, for two reasons: you get a better quality employee for less money (their employment options are more limited), and you can understand each other's language so giving instruction is easier.

This last point is more important that it seems, and although we can speak French and chat away friends all day in grammatically correct French, it is still not fluent enough to be crystal clear, and certainly does not have enough common slang!

Contrat à Durée Déterminée (CDD)

This is a fixed-term contract for a specific duration of employment. There is no minimum time-period, but the length of a CDD should not exceed 18 months, after which the employment should cease or the contract be transferred to a CDI. However, this minor point is not always adhered to on state funded contracts, which strikes many as double standards – but there you are.

The employee's rights and obligations are identical to those of a person with a CDI, and a CDD should only be used in the following situations:

- Seasonal or irregular work such as vegetable harvesting or grape picking, holiday camp or hotel staff.

- To replace an employee who is absent for a prolonged period.

- To accommodate temporary increased staffing needs.

A CDD cannot be given for jobs that are considered dangerous, or where specific skills are required to maintain safety. You will not be the one that judges whether the job was dangerous should there be an accident, and your insurance is certain to have restrictions imposed!

Contract staff, employed through an agency, enjoy conditions that are almost the same as for a CDD, but companies technically should only use temporary employees for short-term activities. The employee is hired and paid for each placement by the agency, and this can be a way around punitive employment restrictions. If you keep using agency staff to fill a position, and change them regularly (both the employee and the agency), any industrial relations problems are likely to be attributed to you as you must obviously be trying to avoid your responsibilities as an employer. The length of any temporary job contract should again not exceed 18 months, though (again) this is open to abuse.

Part time job contracts

This can apply to any employee who works less than 35 hours a week, whether working fixed term or on a CDI. The annual total hours cannot exceed 1,607 which, with typical holidays aside, equates to just less than 35 hours per week. So overtime one month means less hours another. More importantly for employees in the private sector, they must work a minimum of 60 hours a month to benefit from social security benefits. This is an important consideration for them, and for you should you want a 'part-timer'.

A part-time job contract must (again) always be in writing and should mention all the usual contractual information as well as:

- The monthly or weekly amount of hours worked.

- The maximum overtime, remembering the issue of the maximum number of annual hours.

- Weekly or monthly division of work time.

- How hours can be modified to suit both parties.

TERMINATING A CONTRACT

The arrogant boss yelling, "You're fired!" is perhaps not the best way to go about ending someone's contract of employment, regardless of how much you want to do that, or how appropriate you may feel it would be! If you want to fire someone, get advice! Not going about ending a contract of employment in the proper way can be very costly!

Regardless of the type of job contract, the employer has to give the following documents to the employee at the end of the contract:

- A certificate stating position held (*certificat de travail*).

- A document for Assédic, effectively the benefits office, allowing the person to claim unemployment benefits.

It is not easy for employers in difficult times to pay social charges, and several people suspect employers do not always declare their employees to the state – especially if the employee is from a small ethic minority such as the English. While you have the same rights in law as a French employee, this could cause problems, sometimes the employer assuming that you will not go to the authorities to claim benefits.

11

The French banking system

'Rechercher après les sous, et les livres vont s'occuper d'eux-mêmes'

('Look after the pennies, and the pounds will look after themselves')

This chapter of the book gives an introduction to the French banking system, explains some of its idiosyncrasies, gives information on opening a bank account in France (you will need two accounts at least, one personal and one business account), and introduces some of the terminologies used in everyday business life.

Banks are profit making businesses whose sole purpose is to lend you money (for which you pay interest), and provide financial services (for which you pay). They make it as easy as possible for you access their services (for which you pay) and oh yes, they do help you save money ... for which they pay significantly less interest than they charge. The charges for each business or service may be small, but lots of small charges soon add up to a big cost! Looking after the pennies is what they are all about!

Banks typically sell their services as though they are doing you a favour! A classic example is 'Internet Banking'. You are charged for *not* coming to the bank to access your account. If you do come to the bank, it costs them (they need staff, etc.), so to access your account 'online' must save them. So the banks win twice, they let you save them money, then charge you for the privilege! Now this is a good business to be in!

The system of banking in France is in many ways similar to that in England, yet less risky, more personal, polite and with less *obvious* security. It seems that banks treat their clients more like human beings and less a potential thief out to rob the bank! Typically the atmosphere in the bank is more restrained, with easy queues and few people endeavouring to push ahead. The nice thing is that you will be treated like an individual.

There are some drawbacks when dealing with banks in France. The atmosphere can seem almost lax. The problem is best summed up by an old cartoon which depicted a bank queue with everyone covered in cobwebs, their wait had been that long. It can be frustrating as the person in front of you arrives at the counter, and their carrier bag that you had assumed was full of shopping turns out to be full of paper to be pulled out and examined ... each sheet in turn. Then, horror of horrors, you see a baguette hidden and realise they may be there for the duration, they have brought their lunch!

The French do seem prepared to discuss a welter of issues at once, lay siege to the counter, and of course this ensures the tellers know the customers well – and their conversations wander off to matters better dealt with over a coffee or wine at the local café.

If you have no patience, France can be frustrating at times, but then there are many other pleasures that compensate. Plan ahead, get to the bank at 11.45, you can be sure that no-one will want to miss lunch, and you will be surprised how quickly business is dispensed, and queues diminish. What a surprise, by lunchtime the last customer is being hustled out of the back door, as staff eagerly anticipate their lunch!

The less formal approach is no less professional, but occasionally mistakes do get made. An example of this is when, some years ago, we went to our bank. Joining the orderly queue we heard a discussion where the obviously English client was becoming increasingly agitated by the minute. She had no French and the cashier was being talked over by her Manager (a dragon-like lady with few personal skills it seemed), and the discussion was becoming louder by the minute. I went over to see if I could help. That was my first mistake.

The lady depositor pointed to the various piles of cash on the counter. She was sure of the amount she had handed over, and that the wretched bank had lost several hundred Euros. The Manager, fire and brimstone obviously welling up inside her, rose to her full height (even then, not very tall) explaining that the client must obviously be wrong. Of course she (as manager) couldn't possibly make a mistake. Acting as a go-between I explained the various positions and at least extracted a promise from the manager that she would check the cash totals. The depositor was clearly upset, but there remained little else she could do.

Thinking that this was an end to the matter, our business was completed and we went home. A little after 2 pm (lunch always comes first at the bank), we received a call from the bank – a very contrite manager explaining that the money had turned up after all. She could not understand how the money had gone missing, but could I telephone the lady and explain that all was now well. I hastened to remind her that France is a big place, and that I did not know who the heck this woman was just because she was English. England is a big place and we had never met her before. The bank at least knew her name, thought they knew the commune where she had a holiday home, but they could not phone her themselves (she explained) as they had no English. To admit their mistake would, for her, be embarrassing. Luckily I found the lady in question, and gave her the news. All is well that ends well! Did the manager say thanks? What do you think?

There are two issues here: that mistakes get made but that the staff was honest enough to own up. Bank employees are human too, and the teller who was having dreadful difficulty with a client who spoke no French.

The large numbers of English clients have pushed French banks into having more employees who speak English, so communication is much easier. Also, the majority of banks have English language websites and good facilities for the English in many branches. Indeed, because of the large number of English speaking residents and tourists, most hole-in-the-wall cash machines are multi-lingual with English as one of the options. But beware, not all.

MAJOR FRENCH RETAIL BANKS

There are numerous French banks, more than in England where the market is dominated by a few large players on the high street. However, it is hard to know who owns who. Some of the major high street French banking names include:

- **BNP Paribas** (with a website in English). This bank has its own branches, but also runs regional and separate subsidiaries such as the Banque de Bretagne which has a good and visible high street presence almost in competition with the BNP Paribas.

- **Caisse d'Epargne**

- **CIC**

- **Credit Agricole**, one of the world's largest banks and very visible everywhere.

- **Credit Mutuel**

There are French internet banks (which I do not use for preference and security reasons).

Most standard banks do have internet facilities, but with the ever-increase of internet crime and identity theft, I am cautious of any internet banking facility. Equally these services usually cost money! I also know many French people who steer clear of internet banking – perhaps it is a touch 'new'.

Barclays France is one of the few British banks with a French presence, but their presence is limited! A British bank saying "We have a branch in France" sounds good when you are in England, but this can have little or no practical consequences when you are here. France is a significantly bigger country (in area) than England, and simple demographic issues mean you should consider a French bank from day 1.

OPENING AN ACCOUNT

As a foreigner, you may open a French bank account if you are going to be resident in France for more than three months. When starting a business in France, it is obligatory. If you have an account just your business, and all business transactions go through that, for a new, small business, accounting is easy!

You will need certain documents to open an account, France is well known for its need of paperwork:

- **If you are an EU citizen**: Proof of your identity – a valid passport or ID card.

- **If a non-EU citizen**: Proof of residence – a Carte de Séjour entitling you to live in France (this is not an automatic right).

- **Proof of a French address**: a utility bill, an EDF bill is best, rental agreement or your property deeds. It seems perhaps unnecessary, but is typical in France where you need to prove your status. Many people will ask for a utility bill to give proof of your living in a property (you are not a vagabond).

- **Proof of earnings or status**: A contract of employment, proof of earnings and/or proof of status if at all possible. Because of the large number of holiday home owners, this is often ignored!

- **References**, from other banks where accounts are held, if available in the UK, but this is only a realistic option if you are looking for a loan or overdraft.

- In some cases a **birth certificate** or a **marriage certificate** may be asked for, but often if you say these are not available, they *may* be waived!

Opening an account should be done in a day if you are dealing with a senior staff member, and cash cards and cheque books will usually arrive sometime afterwards, probably within a week to ten days of the account being opened – this is a **working** week or up to ten **working** days (i.e. two weeks).

Accounts may be held in joint names, but beware of a minor detail here. An account held by two parties will have the words "et" or "ou" between the names. In the case of an account held in the names M **et** Mme, *both* account holders must sign a cheque, while in the case of an account in the name M **ou** Mme, *either* account holder may sign. Now this should be pointed out to you, but when you are opening the account, make certain you specify which you want!

French banks will, like banks in the UK, charge for certain services, but not all banks have the same charging structure, and different types of account will have different free and chargeable services. When you are opening a bank account these options will generally be made available to you, but with charges explained in French, they may not be clear. Just beware that you do not sign up for services you do not need nor want.

USING YOUR ACCOUNT

Depending on the type of account you choose, a cheque book, and payment and cash withdrawal card, the **carte bleue**, will be issued. Each card has a unique PIN number, and the security system that has been in operation in France for many years is now common in the UK too. The carte bleu can be used extensively, and is good as cash.

The use of credit cards in the UK is taken for granted, where you can get cash from banks, cash machines, and a variety of 'cashback' venues such as supermarkets – everybody wants to be a bank it seems. Here in France your options are more limited.

- You can use cheques anywhere. They are equivalent to cash, and a cheque given cannot be stopped.

- You can use the carte bleu for anything from meals to 24-hr petrol stations, where you either interact with people or automated machines. It is vital you know your PIN number, and validation of the transaction and PIN number is the first step in payment. There are a maximum number of errors you can make before the card is lost to you – they assume if you do not know the PIN you must have stolen the card! Indeed, use of the carte bleu is so common that cash is becoming a rare commodity with some people!

- Do not expect to get cash from anywhere except a bank or cash machine – you will be disappointed as many English tourists find when they arrive on Sunday with no food (the shops are closed) and little petrol! This may change, but it is unlikely as, traditional as always, banks would probably not want others to start muscling in on their territory.

GETTING MONEY TO FRANCE

With the fluctuating value of sterling, and currently the poor exchange rate, any way that you can get more Euros for every pound you bring across must be a good thing. Typically banks offer the service of transferring money. You may find their rates are not competitive compared to internet or specialist providers, so look around.

Some of the issues you will need to bear in mind when changing and transferring money include:

- The exchange rate you are offered will change with the amount you bring across. Smaller amounts warrant poorer rates of exchange.

- Not all banks offer the same rates, and some banks will give you the much better 'Commercial Rate', but perhaps only if you ask them!

- You can use a French bank with a branch in the UK to transfer cash!

- There are two major areas of charges, even just for cash, that can alter the amount you get. One is commission; the other is the exchange rate. It pays to be cautious when people make extravagant claims. The last time I was in the UK, changing some money at the Post Office (no commissions), I received less than at a well-known major store (who gave a much better exchange rate). In their ads, the Post Office imply you will get a better deal with them – just be careful.

- Some money transfer and internet sites will move money and give much better rates of exchange. One such is HIFX. There are others.

Each bank will have a slightly different system, but all you need is a bank in the UK where you have money, and a bank in France to receive the money. These do not need to be the same bank, and the people that exchange the money do not need to be associated with either, so shop around for the best rates.

WRITING FRENCH CHEQUES

When writing or reading French numbers on cheques, it is good to know what the numbers are, how they are written and the placement of points and commas.

- A point marks the thousands, while a comma separates the cents: one thousand Euros is written €1.000,00 or '*mille Euros*'; two thousand is written €2.000,00 or '*deux mille Euros*'.

- A comma marks the fractions in a percentage: fifty-two point six percent is written 52,6%

Now while things like this may seem important, the majority of tellers and other staff in banks and elsewhere are aware that 'the English' do things differently, and other nationalities too, and make errors based on lack of awareness. They will make efforts to read what you write. If you make spelling mistakes, it will probably be overlooked, and except for glaring mistakes cheques will be honoured. However, if you make the mistake of writing too much, and the words agree with the amount you write in numbers, you will end up paying too much! Just be careful!

It still surprises me how difficult some people find this, and how many cheques are ruined. We have had to write out the cheques for some clients! The problem is created (in part) because the cheque is laid out slightly differently. It is largely a simple matter of remembering that the two important lines, how much you are paying to whom, are reversed.

Knowing the numbers and how they are written in French is quite important, and I have seen people (generally older) who find it impossible to write even the basics in French. This puts you at a serious disadvantage, and you lay yourself open to unscrupulous people taking advantage of you! The cents, or centimes as they are still sometimes called, can be written in numbers or as a fraction of 100. This number should correlate with the box for the amount in numbers on the right hand side of the cheque. Please write the numbers clearly, and try to cross the seven in continental style if you remember (**7**). The reason is simple: the French write their number 1 very similarly to the way the English write their 7 – a source of obvious potential confusion.

The second section (normally the third line from the top) is who the cheque is payable to. This section normally has 'à' at the beginning, simply translated as 'to'. There are 3 more bits of information required, all located underneath the box where you write the amount in numbers. The first of these marked 'A' is the place where you wrote the cheque. Nobody will check this, but the line should be filled. The second marked 'Le' is the date the cheque is written, as in England. Because the way the date (in numbers) varies from the English, it is best to write the date, month and year. Again, while months written in French vary from the English some (there are many similarities), why not take the time to learn them in French? If you write it in numbers, tradition has it that the sequence is month, day then year. The final thing is the signature, in the bottom right hand corner.

PAYING BY CHEQUE

Photographic ID (for example passport or sometimes a European style driving license) may be requested when paying by cheque, especially for larger amounts. You should carry a passport, despite being in the EU, as the French carry their ID card! Our company is well known by certain suppliers, and have never had a problem, but each time we must go through the same ritual of proving identity. Paying by personal cheque does not incur additional charges in France; however, a fee can be charged to use a banker's draft for large amounts. This 'Cheque de Banque' is far less common in France in our experience, but this may vary region to region.

Perhaps this is because cheques are treated as a cash payment, French law makes a cheque equivalent to cash, and it is illegal to write a cheque if there are not sufficient funds in the account to cover the payment. This makes for greater security with use of cheques – they do not bounce. Modern life makes this more flexible, and often banks will just cover you if you go a little over the odds, charge you for going overdrawn, and if this happens too often can shout at you and even close your account we understand. If a cheque is written that the bank cannot pay because of lack of funds, the bank is obliged to report it to France's national banking authority, which can forbid the account holder from using cheques for five years. Bad news.

You are not allowed to write a post-dated or open-dated cheque, or receive them in theory. Reality has it that if you are given a post-dated English cheque, some managers will put it in their top drawer until the due date. A post dated French cheque is unusual. A cheque is valid in France for one year and eight days from when it is written, and in this time can only be cancelled if it is lost, stolen or if there is a real suspicion of fraud.

As a cheque book nears completions, the bank will send another one if a form requesting automatic renewal has been filled in. Postal fees are charged for registered delivery. Renewal can also be made by filling in the form provided in a cheque book. Collection can be made at the branch, but give two weeks to allow delivery.

When paying a cheque into the bank you need to sign the back. As a good habit, why not write the number of the account (where you want the money to go to) on the back of the cheque as well. It does mean that, if you have more than one account, fewer mistakes will be made.

RELEVÉ D'IDENTITÉ BANCAIRE (the RIB)

This slip of paper, often supplied in the chequebook (but there are never enough when you start a business, and banks vary as to how many are included), establishes your bank account details and identity. A cancelled cheque can work just as well. It is asked for when you want to open trade accounts, or when you pay via direct debit for regular payments (electric or phone bills for example), or even when people are paying into your account (such as family allowances). It contains the account number (numéro de compte) the bank code (code de l'établissement) and the sort code (code du guichet).

TITRE INTERBANCAIRE DE PAIEMENT (the TIP)

This replaces the use of a cheque when making a payment, is often used by services like telephone and water, and comes attached to the bottom of the invoice (facture). While it makes life easier, some people do not like TIPs, others are very keen. If you do use this system, the first time you receive an invoice, sign it and enclose a RIB in the envelope provided. The next invoice amount will automatically have all the bank information printed on the TIP and needs only to be signed, dated and posted off.

FRENCH BANKING TERMINOLOGY

French banking terminology is something you can get by without, as many bankers now speak at least some English. When you deal with banks, and for important matters, because bank terminology is so complicated and specific you will probably prefer to deal verbally with a manager in a branch who can explain in English. When it comes to fine detail, any contract you have with a bank will be written in French and French legal/banking jargon at that, so the chances of you reading the fine details are limited.

So your need for complex banking terminology is limited to those things you will hear in everyday conversation, or used when you go into a bank. The following list is not expected to be exhaustive, but covers the majority of things you will touch upon.

French Banking terms

Avis d'opération	The slip (normally left on counters that you are expected to fill in) recording the operation carried out on your account, for example depositing cash and cheques.
Chèque	A cheque, a cheque book is called '**un chequier**'. "J'ai besoin d'un autre chequier, s'il vous plait." – "I need another chequebook please."
Code personnel	For online banking: the secret code for access to your account information.
Compte - destinataire	When you are transferring funds, this is the receiving account – the one to which money is being sent, hopefully yours.
Compte inactif	This is an account that has shown no movement for a period of 12 months. Because of the legal issue of honouring cheques, and because cheques are valid for over 1 year, banks prefer to leave accounts open but dormant or inactive.
Compte-joint	This is simply an account in the name of several people allowing each to draw cheques and carry out other bank business. A **Co-joint,** effectively a partner or **Collaborateur** who can be a marital or business partner or just an employee who can be signatories on a joint account.
Crédit	Just as in English, credit is effectively a loan or facility on long or short terms, but is usually used for short term facilities. A loan is called a **prêt**, and an overdraft a **découvert**. (see later for both of these)
Crédit revolving	Revolving Credit! This is a facility that remains constantly topped up to a certain limit even after debits.
DAB	**Distributeur Automatique de Billets**, the equivalent of an Automatic Teller Machine known to many as the

	hole in the wall machine.
Date de valeur	The date at which the bank considers the debit or credit is valid, in other words when the money enters or leaves you account
Date opération	The real date that a debit or credit is made. (The Date de Valeur is determined from this date).
Différé du prêt	This corresponds to the period during which loan (prêt) repayments are temporarily suspended.
Découvert	An overdraft for an agreed period, which can be for as little as 15 days. A **découvert autorisé** is an authorized overdraft, a facility that is charged but where going overdrawn does not cost you every time you make a withdrawal.
Facilité de caisse	This is a short term overdraft facility.
Intérêts	Interest on accounts or loans, it is remarkable how many words are similar in English and French!
Mandataire	Person to whom an account holder gives the power to operate an account in their name, a named signatory.
Mensualité	A monthly payment or repayment.
Prélèvement	An automatic direct debit authorised and signed for by account holder.
Prêt	Is a bank loan, as in **'prêt d'honneur'** (loan on trust), **'prêt personnel'** (personal loan) or **'prêt relais'** (bridging loan). A mortgage is properly called an **'Emprunt'**. The French language can be confusing at times, because the word prêt also means ready, as in **'prêt-à-porter'** which means ready to wear!
Procuration	This is the proxy or power of attorney to carry out bank operations on behalf of someone, but if you need this service, the chances are you are not considering setting up in business!
RIB	Relevé d'Identité Bancaire. We have already discussed this.
Renouvellement automatique	Automatic renewal of your chequebook, this is less automatic than in England in our experience. In England we received a chequebook after writing 'so many' cheques, here you are more likely to be asked to

	send in the slip in your cheque book to order a new one. In our experience, the new cheque book will be sent to the bank, not your home.
Taux	The rate of interest. In many cases for long term loans, the rate of interest is fixed over the duration of the loan, making budgeting easier, and is measurably lower than in the UK. "Why?" one could ask!
TIP	The Titre Interbancaire de Paiement is the authorised permission to debit an account of the sum asked for, as previously discussed.
Titulaire	The account holder, probably you if you are thinking of starting in business.
Versement	The paying a sum of money into an account
Virement	The transfer of a sum of money to another account

If you want or need further information, you can find more on some websites such as AngloInfo.com that specializes in helping the English, or the websites of individual banks.

12

60 ways to improve your profits

"When you lose something, don't lose the lesson.
When you win, never forget it!"

The emphasis of this chapter is all about finding what is right for your business, looking at ideas you could perhaps adopt and personalise, then apply. The objective is to help you improve your business and profits, at any stage of your business life. Always see these in context, and keep the ideas of Breakeven and Gross Margin in mind as you read them. Yes, there are techniques and ideas here that you can adopt to improve your sales, and improve your efficiency, but these may in turn increase your costs and therefore reduce your profits. Ideas should not be taken in isolation, and you should not blindly rush in without considering what the full impact of your choices may be.

Always remember, being in business is all about profits, not just sales.

Moving on from here, like many of the English traders and artisans here in France, you need to consider the wisdom in this chapter, especially in relation to your situation and the environment that you work in.

Whatever you do, start by making a definite decision to improve things. Many people will say they want things to be better, but then will let things slip back to the way they were at the first hurdle. There must be a reason why you want things to improve, and this should be your goal. Set yourself a target, and a timeframe, you then have your objective, your goal. Then you will be set to achieve and move your business forward.

IMPROVE YOUR SALES

1. Define your customers and expand your horizons – too many English artisans and traders concentrate on the British in the community. As 90% of the people in France are French (gosh!), try looking for French clients, look for and point out your advantages. It may be that you start doing this slowly, but working with French clients does bring the advantage that you will improve your language skills, which will improve your confidence. You start a virtuous circle.

2. Offer what customers want – a problem in France is that the French are more conditioned to accepting what they are offered in some areas, sometimes not getting the service they could expect, especially regarding timeliness. This provides a huge opportunity to take advantage of others' weaknesses, and justify your cost! Do not be shy or reticent, and if you are good at something, say so!

3. Reap the referrals, especially those that exist within certain networks such as foreign national groups. These referrals are hot leads, and are an effective introduction to a person who could probably use your services. The benefit to you is that these are easier and less expensive sales because they do not carry the normal costs of selling.

4. Concentrate on existing customers' extended needs, look for other jobs for now or for later. Here in France as elsewhere, once clients have a good supplier, they will tend to stick with them. Finding reliable trades and traders can be difficult! So the more opportunity you can find, the more work there is. As selling costs on average are about 20% of the turnover of your business (when you consider time, as well as all the other costs

associated), you can see that if you can find easier sales, this relative cost is significantly reduced. Reduced costs mean more profit!

Get more from every opportunity. This effectively means making each project or sale bigger, better and more profitable. The first opening or job may be not too interesting, but it could and should lead on to other things.

My first introduction to this was in a consultancy project, when we were required within the early weeks to begin what was known as a 'Scope Chart', which looked at a client company by area, and noted those things where they could have further problems and further work! This then became a regular point of conversation.

It is also demonstrated by a Portuguese lady who runs a clothes shop in Perros Guirec on the North coast of Brittany. When a client enters, looking at a particular item, she is good at making a first sale. She then produces all manner of complimentary items and things to match, and invariably will add one or two items to every sale

5.   Or she will introduce something more expensive, making you want to buy something even more expensive! Notice that she never shows you anything cheaper, understanding that you could obviously afford your first choice! A classic example of another tip, once someone has decided to buy something, tempt them to upgrade what they want!

6.   Have some 'banker' customers (customers who can be relied on for regular, if less profitable work), or regular customers that you treat well! These people help by keeping you busy and helping the flow of cash, and busy people are always preferred to those who have fewer customers. Not busy? Potential customers will wonder why!

7.   'Commissions for referrals'. This is a bit vulgar, but some people would appreciate a thank-you gesture if they have given you a good referral. It should always be retrospective, and not large so as not to appear improper. If you treat people well, they

like it and will treat you well in return. It may be flowers, a meal, or just a bottle of wine, but gestures are appreciated, if done discretely.

8. Perfect the art of Pareto, the 80/20 rule. Most of your sales will come from around 20% of your contacts, as will 80% of your profits. You can improve your sales conversions, and improve your profits, if you can focus on getting more 'good' clients, if you can spot what makes a good client 'good'. You will also avoid wasting time elsewhere.

9. Prune the garden, and lose the clients that always seem to want more for less, cause problems, or that just always complain. Remember the need to cover your costs, and losing customers transfers their share of your fixed costs onto those that remain. Some clients will buy things from you, but cost you money, time and even cause repercussions with other clients. Look carefully at what these clients add to your business. Of course, there may be clients where, for various reasons, you acknowledge you make less money, but you do not mind, friends for example.

10. Quality comes first – in everything. Work well all the time, it saves you money! Poor quality of work and service actually costs you money. So do things right, first time.
    These costs are often hidden, but the cost of poor quality has a significant impact on the bottom line. As an example, let's assume on one project you make 12% net profit on sales of €10,000, giving you a profit of €1,200. Let's also assume your Gross Margin should be 40%, having direct costs of €6,000. Because of poor quality you have to do 25% of the work again, so you will probably have increased your direct costs by 25%, adding another €1,500 to your costs and wiping out your profit. Worse than that, you will also have lost the time that you could have spent on another project earning you (perhaps) another €1,500 profit. So your loss is doubled. Do the job right first time!

11. It pays, when in doubt, to use adequate materials. Poor materials increase problems and repairs, and can even cause multiple efforts to get the job done properly in the first instance! It is not worth the small savings you can make by using cheap materials! As an example, a friend insisted on installing a low-cost toilet for a client, rather than spend twice the amount to purchase elsewhere. The cistern leaked. Trying in vain to increase the pressure on the joint, he cracked the cistern, the toilet then needed to be replaced. This replacement was dropped, breaking the second cistern. The third cistern was OK, but still he had the same leak, so he had to go out and buy a set of quality joints and bolts to hold the cistern to the toilet. The job should have taken 1 day, and cost around €100. Instead, in his efforts to save €40 on the price of the toilet, he bought 3 toilets (cost €180), the extra fittings (€40), it took 4 days, and 3 visits to the low cost supplier. It reminded us of Murphy and the Bricks. He has learned never to do that again!

12. Complaints are an opportunity! Moving on from the last point, how you deal with complaints can create an opportunity. Explaining to a customer why a problem occurred may make you feel better, but it does not really interest the client. They are not really interested in your problems. You have to sort the problem anyway, so why not do it properly, quickly and well, and just say sorry. You may gain!

13. Do you double your advertising budget or make advertising more effective? You could increase the money spent on advertising, but you could perhaps better ask whether the money you did spend worked well for you! Did it bring in enough enquiries? There will always be quiet spells, but you need to make a judgement whether the money spent was money well spent. Simply spending twice the budget with the same media is unlikely to have a proportionate improvement, if any at all.

14. Press coverage – get a trumpet and blow it. The local press in France do run stories about new arrivals and their (unusual) plans for the future. If you do something unusual, provided that

you can interest the press sufficiently to print an article, this is a great way for blowing your trumpet. If this embarrasses you, never fear, smile and enjoy your 15 minutes of fame.

IMPROVE YOUR PRICING

15. It is surprising how few people in business understand their costs and therefore fail to make allowance for them when prices are calculated. Make sure your prices reflect both your costs and your need to make a profit. It is surprising how few people know what their costs actually are when working out their prices, and having competed against some, and been told their charges, they cannot be making a realistic profit. From a competitive point of view, that is OK, because it is their loss. However, from an ethical point of view it is a shame to see a person who will work for little return, or a client who will ultimately be dissatisfied!

16. Price for profit – that does not mean cutting cost to increase sales, nor that your wages are the profit. Remember your advantages; these are not free to the client. Tell clients what you do for them, make it known that this service has value, and make sure that these are considered valuable! Make your prices fair for you too!

17. As you are exporting your services to France, remember that your costs in England, and future costs in France will not be the same, so do your research. The French are very patriotic and prefer to buy from the French, so it they come to you there are things you offer that they cannot get elsewhere. This may be your business idea is novel, your service may be superb, it may be your punctuality, or even that they have fallen out with Pierre who eats too much garlic! It is your decision whether you can or should charge a premium, but it entirely possible!

18. Discounting, or reducing the price, only works for you if your costs go down by at least that amount. Simply reducing your

price because somebody asks for a price reduction is the same as giving away your profits. The two areas where discounting can reasonably be expected are relating to bulk or cash sales. With bulk sales traditionally some form of incentives are given, but these are often linked to advantageous payment schedules and strict drawdowns. Cash sales and black market prices are also expected to be lower because of your savings on TVA (cash sales) and cotisations. But it is a dangerous game, and think carefully before starting.

19. Should you give discounts for early settlement of bills or should there be increases if people pay late? In France, many public companies do charge for late payments. It is not unexpected, and does motivate people to pay on time! You must ensure that the charges are clearly laid out on your terms and conditions. It is always difficult to recommend this, but in some industries, it is more acceptable.

20. A variation on this, especially with industrial clients, is the timing of your invoices. Some companies have a policy not to pay until the third invoice is submitted. Working on the assumption that invoice runs are monthly, they gain 3 months free credit! The big assumption is that invoices are sent monthly. If you were to send invoices more frequently, and mark the third invoice clearly, it may get paid sooner – after all, the accounts staff is only doing what they are told!

21. Get deposits to cover direct costs if this is appropriate. With many English clients away for long periods, and when jobs take many months (therefore tying up finance), it can be hard work to find the cash to outlay for purchases of materials. There are many that charge for material costs up front as a cash deposit, thereby reducing their outflow of funds. Equally important, but naughty, it does provide funds that help you finish other jobs that you have on the go. It is likely that this is why many French firms start projects but do not actually finish them. It is also how people manage to build up the size of contracts they can undertake!

REDUCE YOUR COSTS

22. The first principle of cost reduction is to look for effectiveness and value. If you feel that a substitute product can reduce costs, that is fine but look at the ramifications of buying cheaper.

23. Selection of suppliers and their products is the key to keeping costs low and quality acceptable or better. Remember the trade off between quality, cost and convenience. A supplier may be low cost, but situated many miles away and/or offer poorer quality products. Equally, well publicised offers of cheap lines to entice you into the store may mask higher prices elsewhere or may signify poorer quality or limited guarantees.

24. Convenience costs you money. Local suppliers are often more expensive but cut costs of time and transport, and (especially for small items) expected savings do not justify long trips (journeys in France are deceptively long). Unless you have to visit or pass the areas where the cheaper suppliers are, it may pay to buy local. Of course, it is true that if you are not busy, buy as you think best. That old phrase 'Time is money' is a very true one.

25. Bulk discounts – friend or foe? How many people fall for the offer of bulk discounts? These are generally offered to entice you into a store, or when someone wants to offload large amounts of (often unwanted) stock at a seemingly good price. They do this to improve their cash flow, and in doing so can pass their problem on to you! It ties your cash up! There was one builder I met who boasted a warehouse full of stock, but it never seemed to move, and some of it perished with damp (plasterboard, etc.). Buying at bulk discounts can be good if it is in a line that you use or sell regularly!

    An interesting variation on bulk buying can regularly be found in some French supermarkets. You will have become accustomed to the 'bogof', buy one, get one free. Yes, there are always offers specifying discounts, which can be good value. You will naturally assume that, if you buy larger amounts, you get a bulk discount. In other words it is cheaper. Not always so.

I have come across bulk purchase discounts which actually cost more than single purchases (a deception, you might think, but it happens!). Always check the prices!

26. Read the small print. France is a great country known for sticking to the rules, as long as they want to, and for bending the rules when it suits them. Like others, businesses in France put many conditions in the small print which, because you have signed them, become legally binding. Contracts are in French, so reading the small print may be difficult. The way many overcome this is to ask, if possible in French, if there are any significant catches or problem clauses, and the French then seem almost duty bound to spend hours explaining everything in detail. Just be careful because, like in England, small print can lock you into things that have long term consequences.

27. The question of who authorises expenditure for your business is important. If it is you then you understand the constraints your company is under, and should watch costs accordingly. However, others may not be so careful, and although well meaning, may fall for a good sales pitch or volume discounts thinking that they are doing the right thing. It can be expensive and tie up cash.

28. Check invoices for accuracy – it pays not to be too trusting, and people do make honest mistakes. Mistakes do happen, but once you have accepted an invoice, it can be difficult to get mistakes corrected. Especially the big invoices. It does not hurt to check them for accuracy.

29. Easy targets for saving cost include outsourcing and using sub contractors. In France, because of the high employment costs and huge responsibilities for employing staff, it is often cheaper to have a subcontractor perform certain jobs for you. If you take staff on then you certainly need to have sufficient work for them as well as yourself.

30. Try before you buy. How many times have you had a good idea and felt that a piece of equipment or machinery was vital, only

186

to have it sit gathering dust on the shelves. Unused equipment is a waste, and therefore a cost. If you can, try a piece of equipment before you buy it, see if it is what you thought it would be. Remember, you cannot have everything, and one poor purchase means that you must go without something else!

31. Paying bills – paying late is seen poorly by suppliers. You would react badly, feel your customers were being unfair, and offer them poorer service next time. If a supplier offers you poorer service, this will have the effect of increasing your costs elsewhere. Paying promptly saves you money in the long term, no matter how difficult it may seem at the time!

BUSINESS ISSUES

32. The way to avoid problems with costs is to not get into difficulty in the first place, and that is all about keeping ahead of the game using anticipation, communication and planned action. Keeping ahead of the game is a continual challenge.

33. Minimising the tax bill in France is your responsibility. Setting up in certain areas, especially some rural and agricultural areas in France, means that there are financial (usually tax) incentives. Getting a good accountant helps but they are few and far between, and the responsibility for finding ways to cut your taxes is to do your research and be creative. The logic is to be honest, but remember that 'charity begins at home.'

34. Cotisations. These contributions equivalent to national insurance in England are very expensive, and seriously damage your cash flow. The problem you face is that you will pay cotisations on what you earn, and on any profits that remain, so if you take little salary, you get clobbered on profits. There is a legal way around – this is to have another European company in another country, and work for a branch of that company in France – just enough to get health and social benefits while at the same time paying the minimum level of cotisations possible.

187

35. Accountants and accounting practice in France – who does the accountant work for? Many English accountants working in France understand book-keeping, but are not good with the French systems and laws. What you need is that exception, a French accountant or accountancy practice that has a British view of what you pay them to do – not just fill in the forms but also reduce your tax bill. It is worth asking around. Also, when you find a good accountant, try to work with him or her to achieve what you are looking for, a reduced cotisation and tax bill, and to keep most of your profit.

36. Manage your time. Time is money, so make your time count. Remember Pareto? Yes, you get 80% of the benefit from 20% of the effort, so do not waste time on pointless detail, but by the same token, when you start a job, finish it. Stopping and starting is a most ineffective use of time, and you will continually go over the same ground, time and again, until you put a problem to bed!

37. French lunchtimes can be long and leisurely, with afternoons on a full belly with several glasses of decent wine. Consequently afternoons can be less than energetic. The English too like lunch, sometimes long and leisurely with several glasses of wine, but do not make this the norm when you are working, unless the lunch is taken with the client. Bring shorter breaks into the working day, and use breaks as an opportunity to chat to your client. Be a good listener, and you will find the client indicates areas of more work.

38. Here in France, as elsewhere, there are people who would have you take your eye from business. You need to be disciplined otherwise business issues take a lower priority and profits suffer. These are more numerous than in the UK, and include …

    a. The French administrative system who will want you to work to their schedule.

    b. Friends and relations – you feel obliged to spend time when they come over on holiday, which they will more often because of low cost air travel and because French living seems to have many advantages.

c. Social distractions such as aperitifs with friends, barbecues, or even just lazy family lunches. Plus of course doing up your home in France.

39. See jobs through and finish them – then collect what is due. The temptation is always to start the next job. It looks more interesting, the client is threatening to find someone else, it's raining, whatever the excuse, get the first job done before you start the second if you can. Certain trades are more prone to this than others, including building trades, web designers, and writers but many more are prone.

40. Delegate – if you have a dog, why bark yourself? You probably feel that you are better able to do the work than your assistant, after all, your experience counts. But the flaw in your reasoning is clear. Why have an assistant if you do not use him or her. What else could you be doing? Your assistant will never improve without the opportunity to learn and gain experience. Some people find delegating difficult, but it is something you must learn to do.

41. Manage your debtors – new orders, invoice/payment terms and collecting the money. Money management is very important, and yet many new businesses find it both boring and of low priority. However boring or uninteresting, get it done or delegate it to someone you trust. Our local mayor, a plumber and electrician, is renowned for leaving his bills for years before he collects the money.

42. Working without credit saves money if you can achieve it. Credit and especially unauthorised forms of debt like bank overdrafts and loans are cheaper (it seems) in France than in England, but they still cost you. Work with bank and other balances in the black if at all possible.

43. Don't make things complicated. Use the acronym KISS – Keep It Simple and Straightforward. Complication makes things difficult and costs money. There will always be those who think of fancy solutions, but do not listen. Find a way of doing something that is straightforward. To every problem there will be a simple solution that is best, and usually cheapest.

44. Cash is king – still. While doing things in France using cash (all very legal and proper) is *officially* frowned upon, suppliers and other trades like to receive cash if possible. Always be honest yourself, but what others do is none of your concern really. As long as you have your receipts and invoices in order, you are doing things properly. What other people do is up to them!

45. Do not buy things that you do not actually want and need. Investment from business cash flow is simply a choice of how to spend and distribute your profits. No matter the temptation be careful. Now it is clear that investment is necessary, and certain jobs cannot be done without certain equipment, but choosing to spend your profits, sometimes during the year in which they are made, must be done very wisely.

46. Doing nothing is a business decision. In a range of situations you feel almost compelled to do something. With the benefit of hindsight you would have been better advised to do nothing, and the problem would go away. Getting involved in things where you should not costs you money.

    This applies also to things that others would have you do for them. There are many who like to transfer responsibilities onto others, and would have you do for them the things they should be doing for themselves. It is especially prevalent amongst children and family. If you are the type that can be relied upon, then others will want to rely upon you rather than rely upon themselves. It distracts you, wastes time, and gives you responsibilities that take you away from the responsibilities of the business.

47. Manage risk and plan for problems. The essence of business planning is that you consider the way forward rather than just rush headlong into difficult situations. It is generally accepted that considering where the problems may be helps you to avoid them in the first place.

48. Money is not everything – what about customer complaints, late deliveries, poor conversion of sales leads, poor quality workmanship, staff turnover, breakdowns, and customer satisfaction. Putting too much focus on just the financial consequences of decisions may mean that you reach the wrong conclusion. Staff turnover, breakdowns or anything that disrupts progress or costs time or work must, by definition, cost you money!

PROFESSIONAL ADVICE

49. Professional advisers – choose wisely and take advice when you need it. However, remember that not all advice is good or even appropriate! Every adviser believes they can contribute in some way to the dilemma you face. For example, a sales consultant could help improve profitability, which is true. But just increasing sales may create problems elsewhere as we have seen, which could equally reduce profitability (or worse).

50. Make things easy for advisers and accountants. It may seem silly to say this, but advisors in any field try to be focused, professional and economical with their time. They have no wish to talk about your family or indeed anything else ... unless it has a bearing on what they are doing. Consequently anything that wastes their time has two effects – it upsets the advisor (so you get less help), and it costs you more! Keep things focused!

When something is important, and questions are asked that you may find embarrassing, answer then openly and honestly. Unless you do, any advice will be poorer as a result. It is always better to be truthful. Unfortunately many people are clever enough to see where a series of questions is going, and try to put the blame elsewhere to save embarrassment. You may ask who is being fooled, the advisor or the client!

BANKS

51. Choosing the right bank is important. This may sound silly, but there is an important point here. If you are in business, or even just starting, you need a bank that will listen to what you want, and will react accordingly. Some banks tend to make less effort to know and understand you. You matter less to the banks who try to spend less by using inexperienced people to deal with your request. They tend to be younger and less able to judge you or your proposition.

52. Get your bank to say yes, by giving them reasons to support you. Lending to small businesses is as much based on you, and the bank's belief in you, as anything else. You should know your business, and if you have done your business planning well, will have probably thought of all angles. If not, be honest; remember that bank managers are human too and like to feel as though they have made a positive contribution to your business. Bank employees are generally nice people, and while they generally do not have the independence of spirit to start for themselves (unless they are exceptional or it is forced upon them), they do like to feel that they have something to offer you and your business, and want to be helpful.

53. Reducing the costs of banking is always important. There are two main ways this can be achieved:

    a.   Minimise the amount you need from the bank.

    b.   Find the cheapest way of doing things.

Banks do provide a necessary service, but that service is not free, and you should be selective how you use the services they offer, as they would be selective if they use yours. Bank profits are generally huge. Unless they get careless, as with the credit crunch when sheer greed got the better of them! Their motto of looking after the pennies should be made to work for you. €1 saved here, another there, and soon you add a big sum to your profits by taking it off your costs.

IN GENERAL

54. Work to continually improve your image. If your image is poor or unprofessional, the amount you can charge will be less. Your costs will, however, be the same. Hence your profits must (by definition) be lower. The better your image, the better your prices can be. This though is a double edged sword because, as your image improves, so people's expectations of the service you offer will increase. You do end up on a virtuous circle where things get better, rather than a vicious circle where things go from bad to worse!

55. Don't overlook details; the devil as always is in the detail, and so are the problems and the hidden costs. When you sign a contract, check the details carefully. Normally there are no problems, but you may unfortunately get a client who will hold you to contract in an effort not to pay. Or you may find others blame you for their inability to keep to their contract. It can prove expensive.

    One way of avoiding problems is to understand what it is that the client feels is most important, and ensure this is kept in mind. Then, as you are progressing, keep the client informed of what you are doing if appropriate, so that they do not have nasty surprises!

    For larger undertakings such as building projects, this can be easier than it first seems, and listening when the client talks is important. For smaller items, say in a café or a shop, again it is easier than it appears. You set out with principles in mind, a standard that you want to live up to. If you do, then people's expectations will be met, and the experience of using you will be good.

    On a note of caution, there are clients who seem unnaturally interested in the detail. We had one such, a gentleman (let's call him Mr S) who wanted all details spelled out, and continually altered them slightly where the changes could have expensive consequences. Having started wanting a contract in English, he then wanted a contract in French. Despite our having invested time and effort, we walked away from the job believing that we would be held to the detail as an excuse for not paying. There are people in this world, in England and in France, who do not enter into the spirit of a contract, and who have few commercial morals. Fortunately they are few and far between, but they do exist. Let your instincts guide you, and if you are unhappy dealing with someone, walk away!

56. Being different and better makes you memorable. This can only help is any aspect where you are dealing with people, and is especially true where there is competition, for example the high street. The trick is as much in *being seen* to be different, as people will take an interest in what you are doing. It can only help sales, and consequently profits.

    A good example of what this means happened locally. Within weeks two restaurants were sold, around 4 km apart. These were respectively 'Chez Sylvie' and 'La Forge'. Chez Sylvie had always been busier. Both restaurants have very visible positions on a busy road, and both aim for similar customers, catering mainly for the lunchtime trade. The new proprietors of Chez Sylvie kept to the same formula, little changed, whereas the new proprietors of La Forge started improving everything. The bar was cleaned, the front of the building was painted, the menu was changed and the back of the building prepared as a terrace. People stopped to look. They tried the food which is excellent. They found good service, keen prices, and a nice setting. So they came back, and soon the car park at Chez Sylvie was empty at lunchtime and La Forge is packed. Only then did Chez Sylvie make an effort, but it was too late. Their property is now up for sale again!

57. If you want to do business with the French, then you need to understand their priorities to profit from them.

One example of this is in a small town locally. An Englishman has opened a satellite/TV business, with the adjoining shop selling computers and peripherals for the English speakers. About 50 meters away is a small shop, owned by a Frenchman, who also sells satellite dishes. No doubt the English shops would like to benefit from French customers. A French friend locally asked if they realised that no French person would go in when they could go to a Frenchman just down the road. Our satellite salesman and computer business could have picked a better location where they could also have gained French customers. The French are very patriotic and will support French businesses first he explained! And why not! Perhaps it would be better if in England we did the same.

58. Speak the language. Trying to make headway in France, and with the French market, it pays well to be seen to be making an effort. If nothing else, French clients will appreciate your efforts, and you will have opened doors. What you do then is up to you. I cannot see that your business could suffer!

59. In a land where there are many English people trying to run businesses, try thinking outside of the box. Look for new ways to approach a situation. Be creative, and perhaps look for opportunity from new technology. Recently at the Bio fair in Mur de Bretagne we saw many people who are keen to appeal to people looking for alternative approaches to house-building, furnishing, heating and energy, cooking and a plethora of other things. You may already be in business, but looking for creative ideas may open routes where you can improve profits.

60. Then plan your action for improvements. Many people will discuss current issues of business or have ideas of things we should do. These are discussed and then forgotten about. Typical, and what a waste. So when you have decided what you are going to do, write it down with the key steps you will take and when things will be done. Using this as a basis, you can then sit quietly on a regular basis and go through your planned action to review progress.

The logic behind this is simple. When something is written down it assumes far greater importance and you will remember and note other points. Finally, having regular review you keep this as a priority, it does not slip a day or two, and you will make sure things get done – to save the embarrassment of admitting you have done nothing!

It is an old trick, but it works every time. Write it down and things get done. That is why it is called simply ... your action plan!

A final word

Starting a business is, for many, the only way forward and gives you back your self-esteem. For many in society, pressure and the drive for profits, the need for change and the ever-increasing pace of technology, the reducing value from employment and the de-personalisation of work has meant that as you mature, your options of employment get fewer. Your life's dreams become less attainable.

But that does not mean that we do not have dreams, things we want to do, places we want to go, experiences we want to have. What it does mean is that we have to take responsibility for our dreams ourselves. Nobody will do it for you; you have to do it yourself.

Perhaps you lack confidence – we all do at times, but it is then that we have to look within ourselves and find the courage in the person that has for many years may have been held back. If I may, I would like to recount a personal story.

Many years ago I was working in Saudi Arabia as an engineer. One evening, fed up with being away from home for about six months, I found myself speaking to Frank, my boss. He said that he would like to do an MBA. At that time I did not really know what was involved, but hearing what was involved, it sounded interesting and exciting, a good challenge. I said that I would like to do something like that. Remember, at this time I had no qualifications to speak of, but had got where I was by hard work and application. Frank's reply stung me. "You will never be able to do that!" he said, without really thinking how fundamental his words were. I can trace the way my subsequent career to this stray remark. If he didn't think I could do it, I'd show him, and I'm willing to bet that I got there before him.

The motto to this story is that I believe that if you set your mind to do something, you can achieve whatever you want. You are capable of great things, it would surprise you.

There was a phrase I once heard, that I really agree with. Love life deeply and passionately, and let that passion show and you will get so much more from life. Perhaps the saddest phrase I have ever heard was, "I wish I had tried!" Nobody will do it for you. You need to live your life yourself. You might get hurt along the way, but it's the only way to live life completely. Sure, you may get knocks, you may find times hard, but when the going gets tough, as they say, the tough get going!

As long as you have learned from your experiences, and take that knowledge into the future, you cannot have failed. Frank Sinatra once sang of hard times when, if you face big odds and you seem not to be making progress, you need to 'Pick yourself up, dust yourself off, and start all over again.' Indeed, there may be times when things do not work out as you had hoped, but that is never the end of the story, just the beginning of the next chapter.

If you wish to come to France and start a business, or you are already here and want to do better, all the very best. If this book has helped, that will have made the effort of writing it worthwhile. All that is left to say is,

Bonne Chance, et à bientôt!

Index